ISBN: 978-0-578-56557-6

Tastefully Under Pressure

70+ Wholesome Recipes for Stove & Electric Pressure Cookers and Multi-Cookers

Plus Slow Cooking Recipes from Zavor's Test Kitchen

Laura D.A. Pazzaglia

HIP COOKING | www.hipcooking.com

Table of Contents

DISCLAIMER: All recipe information in this book is to be used at one's own discretion. These recipes have been carefully developed to provide result accuracy, however the creators and chefs behind them, as well as Zavor, assume zero responsibility for user error or omission. Please use all information at your own risk; every circumstance and result is unique and will not be a replica of the examples in this book.

Introduction

Zavor is the inspired creation of the team behind Fagor America. After closing its doors, the minds behind the top pressure cooker brand in the country put all their efforts into continuing the product line on their own terms, enter Zavor.

We at Zavor have curated a culinary collection for the contemporary home cook, focusing on easy-to-use tools that bring users closer to that healthier lifestyle we all want to achieve. Our unique products offer a simple and healthy approach to cooking that allows users to create a delicious array of meals that are sure to bring family and friends together. From the novice home cook to the expert chef, all walks of life will benefit from Zavor's versatile collection of trustworthy kitchen tools.

About Laura Pazzaglia

Laura Pazzaglia is the founder of the pressure cooking website Hipcooking.com and has written two books on pressure cookery: The Everything Healthy Pressure Cooker, Hip Pressure Cooking: Fast, Fresh & Flavorful and is working on her third in addition to writing for several top-notch culinary websites.

Laura does more than write & test recipes, her books and articles explore the mechanics of pressure cooking, how ingredients react under pressure, and the nutritional benefits of pressure cooking - one of her pieces has a citation in the scientific literature. She is an industry-recognized expert in pressure cookery serving as a consultant for manufacturers worldwide and performing demonstrations for them in various cities in the United States, United Kingdom, Canada, Germany, Italy, and Luxembourg.

She is credited for starting the pressure cooking egg craze back in 2011- when she figured out the cooking time and technique for steaming eggs in the pressure cooker and found that it made them easy-to-peel. Her experiments brought many pressure cooker first recipes and techniques including al dente pressure cooker pasta and sauce, potato salad that holds its shape, chicken and rice cooked to perfection, a delicious hot sauce plus many more.

Laura enjoys sharing what she has learned in her 15 years of pressure cooking research and experimentation to enable home cooks to improvise their own or follow her no-fail recipes which are guaranteed to succeed in both stovetop and electric pressure cookers.

She has appeared in several infomercials and pressure cooker demonstration videos. But, mostly, she enjoys teaching pressure cooking classes and doing live product demonstrations where cooks can see & taste the benefits of pressure cooking. She produced a free video series, Pressure Cooking School, to reach and teach more home cooks the ease of pressure cookery.

Currently, Laura lives in Italy near Rome and frequently travels to the United States and around Europe to share her passion for kitchen technology. Previously, she was an information technology professional in the San Francisco Bay Area - California's Silicon Valley.

Pressure Cooker 101

What are the Benefits of Pressure Cooking?

Fast. Reduces cooking time by up to 70% when compared to traditional cooking methods.

Easy. Just add the ingredients and cooking liquid into the cooker, close the lid, bring to pressure and cook, then release and open the lid. It's that simple!

Healthy. Because foods are cooked under pressure, up to 50% more vitamins and minerals are retained. Also, shorter cooking times retain more nutritional values of food.

Safe. Zavor pressure cookers, both stovetop and electric, have safety valves that allow any excess pressure to escape, so the cooking experience is entirely secure.

Versatile. Almost all types of foods can be cooked in a pressure cooker – from vegetables to rice to chicken, meats & even desserts.

Energy Efficient. Because pressure cooking reduces cooking times, you spend less time and resources, translating to the conservation of energy.

Delicious. The steam created inside the pressure cooker breaks down the food fibers in very little time, leaving food tender and succulent, with a beautiful intermingling of flavors.

Pressure cookers are great to use all year round!

- **Spring:** Pressure cooking retains the natural color and flavor of foods, allowing you to enjoy all of the vibrancy that fresh, spring vegetables have to offer.
- **Summer:** Because foods are cooked under pressure, your kitchen won't become excessively hot.
- **Fall and Winter:** Comfort food classics and one pot meals made easy! Cook a hearty delicious soup, zesty chili or savory stew in almost no time at all!

How does my pressure cooker work?

When the lid is closed correctly and locked onto the cooker pot, an airtight seal is created. As the food and liquid inside the cooker become hot, the internal cooking temperature reaches up to 250°F. Steam is then generated, and the pressure begins to rise. If you have a Zavor model that has multiple pressure settings (or levels), the cooking temperature reached inside the stovetop models will vary depending on the pressure setting you've selected.

What are the benefits of having two pressure settings?

Depending on the type of Zavor model you have, pressure levels may be indicated with numerical markings (1 - LOW/8psi and 2 - HIGH/15psi) or the words "HIGH" and "LOW". While other stovetop models with one pressure setting will simply say "PRESSURE", which will be the HIGH setting /15psi. Electric models will have dual pressure settings embedded into the control panel - LOW/4-7psi and HIGH/10-13psi.

Before you begin pressure cooking.

It's essential to check all the parts of your Zavor pressure cooker each time you use it. Here's what to check:

1. Make sure the cooking pot is washed well after the last use. There should be no food particles or residue on the pot or lid. Make sure the inner part of the lid rim, the outer rim on the pot, and the rubber gasket are clean. This will reduce the risk of the lid sticking when you open the cooker.
2. Remove and check the gasket to make sure that it's still flexible and not dried out. Check for any tears or cracks. If the gasket shows any sign of being damaged or dry, do not use the pressure cooker. Replace it with a new gasket immediately. A replacement gasket can be ordered by telephone at 855-928-6748 or online at www.zavoramerica.com.
3. Check all the safety valves. Remove the pressure regulator knob and check for any food particles that may be inside from previous use. Since each pressure cooker design is different, check your user's manual for the correct cleaning and maintenance instructions.

LOADING THE PRESSURE COOKER

Because a pressure cooker needs room for pressure to build, never fill your cooker more than 2/3 full. Never fill more than half full when cooking foods that expand when cooked like rice. All Zavor units have a MAX Fill line inside the pot.

Browning meats before cooking adds flavor to the dish as well as extra color. Always brown with the lid off and, if using a stovetop unit, over medium-high or high heat. Be careful that the burner is not too high or you will burn the oil and scorch the pot.

When steaming foods, lightly coat the steamer basket you are using with cooking spray. Foods like fish have a tendency to stick to the surface. When done steaming, remove the food from the steamer basket immediately.

Positioning and Locking the lid in place.

Once all of the ingredients, including food and liquid, are in the cooker, you can begin cooking.

STOVETOP UNITS.

To close the lid, align the arrow on the lid (located to the left of the handle) with the arrow on the base handle. Press down lightly on the lid and turn it clockwise until the two handles line up. You will hear a "click" as the automatic lock locks in place. If your model has top knob handle rather than one main handle, like the EZLock Pressure Cooker, you can place the lid on the pot at any position and turn the top knob to the "closed" position. Next, turn the pressure valve to select the correct pressure setting. Specific models allow you to choose between two levels of pressure (High/Low). Other models only have a High pressure setting.

ELECTRIC UNITS.

To close the lid, align the locking pin on the lid (located at the end of the handle) with the unlocked lock icon on the base (this can be found right above the condensation collector). Press down lightly on the lid and turn it counterclockwise toward the locked lock icon. You will hear a "click" as it locks in place. Next, turn the pressure valve to select the Pressure setting.

Building pressure - Stovetop.

To build pressure in a pressure cooker, the liquid inside the pot must be brought to a boil with the lid locked in place. When the liquid boils, steam is produced, and pressure is created. When using a stovetop pressure cooker, once the lid is securely locked into place, raise the burner to high heat*. As soon as the cooker reaches pressure, the indicator will rise. Once the selected pressure is reached, a small amount of steam will come out of the pressure valve. Once the steam comes out of the valve you must lower the heat on the burner and start timing your recipe. Do not reduce the heat too much; otherwise, the internal temperature will drop, and the steam and pressure will be lost.

*** For electric stove users:**

The coils on an electric stove retain heat for a long time, often causing food to overcook when the burner is turned down (when cook time is started). To avoid this, two burners should be used – one on high heat to bring the unit to pressure, and the other on medium so the cooker can be moved over when the cooking time is started.

Building pressure - Electric.

To build pressure in an electric pressure cooker, the liquid inside the pot must be brought to a boil with the lid locked in place. When the liquid boils, steam is produced, and pressure is created.

When using an electric pressure cooker, once the lid is securely locked into place, select your pressure level, and program your cooking time on the panel. Once the pressure has been reached, the floating valve inside the lid will rise and a small amount of steam will come out of the pressure regulator knob.

Once the pressure has been reached, the internal components of the cooker will automatically maintain the pressure, and the recipe time countdown will begin.

Timing your recipe.

The amount of time you cook food is essential to achieving the best results.

Stovetop: We recommend you have a timer of some sort on hand. Once the desired level of pressure has been reached, set your timer, lower the heat on the burner, and begin your cooking time.

Electric: All timing is done automatically when using an electric pressure cooker, just be sure to follow the recipe or time recommendation properly.

Because overcooked food cannot be corrected, it's better to cook unfamiliar foods for a shorter time. You can always go back and cook foods a little longer if necessary.

Using a pressure cooker at high altitudes.

If you are cooking at a high altitude, the cooking times will be longer, as water and cooking liquids come to a boil more slowly. A rule of thumb to remember is to increase the cooking time by 5% for every 1,000 feet above the first 2,000 feet over sea level (ex: 3,000 feet above sea level, add 5% to cooking time; 4,000 feet, add 10%; and so on).

Since cooking times increase at altitudes higher than 2,000 feet, you will also need to add more cooking liquid to compensate. There are no exact rules for this, so try increasing the cooking liquid by approximately half the percentage of the additional cooking time. For example, if the cooking time is increased by 10%, you will need to increase the cooking liquid by 5%.

Releasing pressure.

When the food has finished cooking, remove the pressure cooker from the burner (only necessary for stovetop units). Although you are no longer cooking, the steam inside the cooker is still extremely hot, and foods will continue to cook until the pressure has been released.

There are two different ways to release cooking pressure in a pressure cooker:

1. **NATURAL-RELEASE METHOD.** To use this method, remove the cooker from the burner or shut it completely off if using an electric model. This method can take anywhere from 10 to 20 minutes, depending on the cooker model and how much food there is inside.
2. **AUTOMATIC PRESSURE RELEASE METHOD.** The pressure regulator knob, available on all types of pressure cookers, allows for an instant release of pressure. Simply turn the knob to the pressure release position and let all the pressure escape, making sure to angle the stream of pressure away from yourself and others.

Opening the pressure cooker.

On all Zavor pressure cooker models, both stovetop and electric, the pressure cooker can only be opened after all the internal pressure has been released. As a safety feature, all units have a safety lock that prevents the cooker from being opened while there is pressure inside.

Since the food in the pressure cooker is extremely hot, use caution in opening and removing the lid. After releasing all the pressure, unlock the lid (if necessary) and turn the lid to open. Even though there is no further pressure in the cooker, there will be some hot steam rising out. To avoid being burned, never hold your face over the pressure cooker as you remove the lid.

Cleaning the pressure cooker.

Stovetop. After each use, wash the inside and outside of the pot and lid with mild dish soap and a non-abrasive sponge, then rinse thoroughly. The pot is dishwasher safe for easy cleaning; however, you should never wash the lid or the gasket in the dishwasher. When cleaning the lid, always remove the gasket and wash it with mild dish soap. After washing, dry all parts of the pressure cooker and place the gasket back into the lid.

Electric. Carefully lift the removable cooking pot and wash it with mild dish soap. The cooking pot is the only part that's dishwasher safe. If you need to clean the actual cooker itself, you can use a damp cloth to wipe the outside and around the rim. Wash the silicone gasket with warm soapy water. Before putting the gasket back onto the lid, make sure that it's completely dry.

Remove the pressure regulator knob to check that there are no bits of food stuck in it. Push down on the knob, turn to the clean setting, and carefully lift up. Run the knob under water to clean any particle build-up inside. To put the pressure knob back into place, line it back up with the clean setting and turn it back to the pressure or steam release setting.

IMPORTANT.

When storing the stovetop units, never lock the lid in place, since you can damage the gasket or worse yet, not be able to reopen the pressure cooker – moisture that may develop can create an almost permanent seal. Always store the lid upside down on top of the pot.

Help is only a phone call away.

If you have questions regarding the use and care of your Zavor pressure cooker, electric pressure cooker or electric multi-cooker, please call our Customer Service Department at 1-855-928-6748 or e-mail us at info@zavoramerica.com.

Accessories and parts.

All available for purchase at www.zavoramerica.com.

Stovetop.

Home Canning Kit: Preserve your favorite fruits, vegetables, & meats safely and efficiently using your Zavor pressure cookers.
Steamer Baskets: A useful accessory for vegetables and other healthy steamed recipes.
Replacement parts: Replacement handles, valves, gaskets, and more.

Electric.

Removable Cooking Pots: Stainless steel and ceramic-coated pots to suit your cookware preferences.
Steamer Baskets: A useful accessory for vegetables and other healthy steamed recipes.
Replacement parts: Replacement valves, gaskets, power cords, and more.

Chapter One

BREAKFAST

Preparing breakfast in a pressure cooker is a great and fast way to make the most important meal of the day. If you have an electric pressure cooker, you can program the Time Delay and have breakfast waiting by the time you wake up!

Classic Steel Cut Oats

BREAKFAST

If using an electric pressure cooker, this recipe can be prepared the night before and the delay timer set to begin cooking before you wake up.

Stovetop & Electric Pressure Cook Time
3 minutes HIGH

Serves
1

Accessories
Steamer basket & trivet, heat-proof container

INGREDIENTS:

¼ cup quick-cooking steel-cut oats
¾ cup water
1 pinch salt
½ tablespoon butter
1 teaspoon raw demerara sugar

DIRECTIONS:

1. Add 1 cup of water to the cooker, insert the trivet and steamer basket.
2. In a small heat-proof bowl or mug, add the oats, water, salt, and butter. Mix well. Lower the bowl into the cooker, close the lid and set the valve to the pressure position.

   Stovetop & Electric Pressure Cook Time:
   3 minutes HIGH

3. When time is up, open the pressure cooker using the natural release method. Electric pressure cookers: Turn off the Keep Warm function and wait until the pressure indicator has gone down (about 20 to 30 minutes). Stovetop pressure cookers: Move the cooker off the burner and wait for the pressure to come down on its own (about 10 minutes).
4. Vigorously mix the contents of the bowl, sprinkle with sugar and serve.

Recipe Tip:
If you prefer to use conventional steel-cut oats, increase the pressure cooking time to 15 minutes for electric and 12 minutes for stovetop.

No-fuss Apple & Cinnamon Rolled Oats

Apple chips to the rescue for when you're not up to peeling and cutting an apple first-thing in the morning!

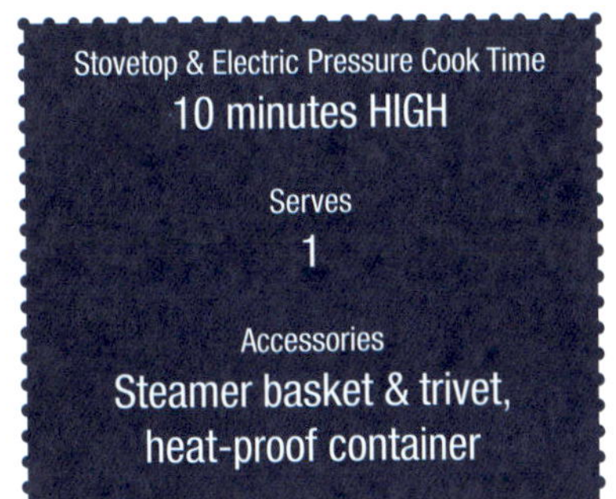
Stovetop & Electric Pressure Cook Time
10 minutes HIGH

Serves
1

Accessories
Steamer basket & trivet, heat-proof container

BREAKFAST

INGREDIENTS:

⅓ cup rolled oats
⅔ cup whole milk
2 tablespoons crumbled dried apple chips
1 pinch salt
1 tablespoon raisins
¼ teaspoons cinnamon powder

DIRECTIONS:

1. Add 1 cup of water to the cooker, insert the trivet and steamer basket.
2. In a small heat-proof bowl or mug, add the oats, milk, apples, salt, raisins, and cinnamon powder. Mix well. Lower the bowl into the cooker, close the lid and set the valve to pressure position.

   Stovetop & Electric Pressure Cook Time:
   10 minutes HIGH

3. When time is up, open the pressure cooker using the natural release method. Electric pressure cookers: Turn off the Keep Warm function and wait until the pressure indicator has gone down (about 20 to 30 minutes). Stovetop pressure cookers: Move the cooker off the burner and wait for the pressure to come down on its own (about 10 minutes).
4. Vigorously mix the contents of the bowl, sprinkle with sugar and serve.

Recipe Tip:
You can substitute the crumbled dried apple chips in this recipe with your favorite dried or frozen fruits.

Blueberries & Cream Oat Groats

You don't have to wait for blueberries to come into season, use the freeze-dried ones. Because of the milk in this recipe, it cannot be set to cook later with the "delay" timer. If you'd like to anyway, substitute the milk with additional water.

Stovetop Pressure Cook Time
28 minutes HIGH

Electric Pressure Cook Time
20 minutes HIGH

Serves
1

Accessories
Steamer basket & trivet, heat-proof container

INGREDIENTS:

⅓ cup oat groats, rinsed
⅓ cup vanilla soy milk
2 tablespoons freeze-dried blueberries
1 pinch salt
½ teaspoon raw sugar

DIRECTIONS:

1. Add 1 cup of water to the cooker, insert the trivet and steamer basket.
2. In a small heat proof bowl or mug, add the groats, soy milk, blueberries, and salt. Mix well and lower the bowl into the cooker. Close the lid and set the valve to the pressure position.

   Stovetop Pressure Cook Time:
   28 minutes HIGH

   Electric Pressure Cook Time:
   20 minutes HIGH
3. When time is up, open the pressure cooker using the natural release method. Electric pressure cookers: Turn off the Keep Warm function and wait until the pressure indicator has gone down (about 20 to 30 minutes). Stovetop pressure cookers: Move the cooker off the burner and wait for the pressure to come down on its own (about 10 minutes).
4. Vigorously mix the contents of the bowl, sprinkle with sugar and serve.

No-pectin Strawberry Jam

This is an old-fashioned no-pectin added jam. It will reduce and become dark and tarty in addition to sweet. When pressure cooking fruit, do not fill the pressure cooker more than half-way. You can use less sugar - however, the jam will not be sweet enough to remain shelf-stable after processing and should be stored in the refrigerator.

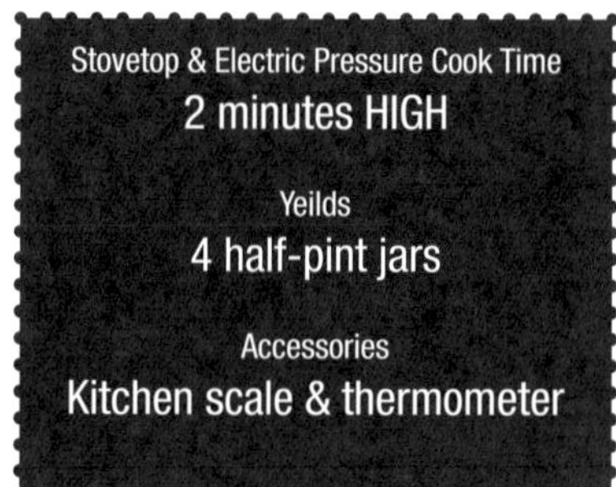

INGREDIENTS:

2 pounds strawberries, cored and halved about
1½ pounds sugar

DIRECTIONS:

1. Place the pressure cooker, or inner pot, on your scale and tumble in the trimmed strawberries. Note the weight. Add ¾ of the weight in sugar, you can use a calculator and multiply the weight your scale reads by .75. For example, for the 942 grams of strawberries, we need just 707g of sugar (942 x 0.75 = 706.5).
2. Then, hit "Tar" or "0" on your scale and pour the sugar in the cooker until you reach the amount you calculated for it.
3. Put the cooker on low heat (Keep Warm function for electric cookers) and occasionally stir until the sugar has liquefied (about 3 minutes). Turn up the heat to high (Sauté function for electric cookers), and stirring occasionally wait for the contents to boil.
4. Close the lid and set the valve to the pressure position.

   Stovetop & Electric Pressure Cook Time:
   2 minutes HIGH

5. When time is up, open the pressure cooker using the natural release method. Electric pressure cookers: Turn off the Keep Warm function and wait until the pressure indicator has gone down (about 20 to 30 minutes). Stovetop pressure cookers: Move the cooker off the burner and wait for the pressure to come down on its own (about 10 minutes).
6. Remove the lid and bring the contents back up to a boil on medium heat (Sauté function for electric cookers) until the mixture reaches 220°F. This step will take about 10 to 15 minutes.
7. Pour hot jam into sterilized, or freshly dish-washed, jars. Carefully clean the edges and top with sterilized lids. Refrigerate for 4-6 weeks.

Lime Marmalade with Fresh Mint

Stovetop & Electric Pressure Cook Time
10 minutes HIGH

Makes
2 cups

Accessories
Mandolin, kitchen scale

This recipe can be adjusted for the number of limes you have since the sugar is decided on the weight of the lime rinds and pulp. Serve with cheese, on crackers, with meat or as the usual breakfast jam!

INGREDIENTS:

2 pounds organic limes, well-washed with a scrubby sponge
About 4 pounds sugar (see instructions)

DIRECTIONS:

1. Slice the limes using the "thin" setting on a mandolin. Stack slices, removing seeds as you go (save them for later) and cut into four.
2. Put your pressure cooker, or inner pot, on your scale, hit "tar" or "0" and then add thinly sliced lime wedges and any juice that may have squirted out in the process. Write down the weight of the fruit (for example 786 grams).
3. Add about 1-2 cups of water to the cooker. Close the lid and set the valve to the pressure position.

   Stovetop & Electric Pressure Cook Time:
   10 minutes HIGH

4. When time is up, open the pressure cooker using the natural release method. Electric pressure cookers: Turn off the Keep Warm function and wait until the pressure indicator has gone down (about 20 to 30 minutes). Stovetop pressure cookers: Move the cooker off the burner and wait for the pressure to come down on its own (about 10 minutes).
5. Calculate how much sugar to add - typically an extra-bitter marmalade needs twice the sugar. That looks like A LOT of sugar if you've never made fruit preserves! So if you are concerned, try the same weight in sugar first, then taste a cooled sample on a teaspoon and see if you like it.
6. Put all the lime seeds in a tea ball or gauze packet. When you open the pressure cooker the fruit pulp will already be warm, so pour all of the sugar in and stir. It should all melt within a minute or two. Then, add the tea ball containing the seeds.
7. Turn the heat up and bring everything to a rolling boil for 5 minutes or, if you have a thermometer, you will want the mixture to reach 212°F. Using a ladle or canning funnel, distribute the contents evenly in your freshly dish-washed or sterilized jars.
8. Serve with cheese and crackers or as you would any standard marmalade. Add a pinch of salt and freshly torn mint leaves before serving. Refrigerate for 1 week, or process in a hot water bath canner following their recommendations to make the marmalade shelf-stable.

Ham & Cheese Egg Cups

When following the steps in this recipe the center of the egg remains somewhat soft – if you would like it fully cooked, simply don't cover with tin foil.

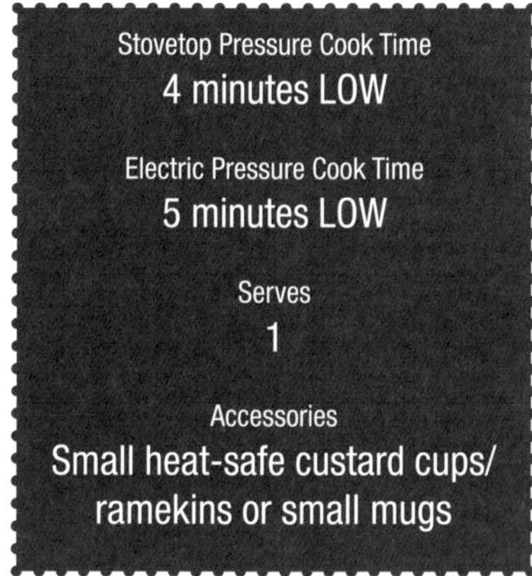

INGREDIENTS:

4 eggs
4 slices ham
4 pinches salt
4 pinches pepper
1 tomato chopped, for garnish
4 tablespoons grated cheddar cheese

DIRECTIONS:

1. Add one cup of water to the cooker and set aside.
2. Lay a slice of ham in each ramekin with the edges sticking up. Break an egg and drop it into each ramekin and then sprinkle it with salt, pepper, and cheddar cheese.
3. Cover tightly with foil and lower the ramekins directly into the water in the cooker. Close the lid and set the valve to the pressure position.

   Stovetop Pressure Cook Time: 4 minutes LOW

   Electric Pressure Cook Time: 5 minutes LOW

4. When time is up, release the pressure and open the lid. Remove the ramekins carefully and serve immediately on a little plate or saucer.

Recipe Tip:
You can vary this quick breakfast with your favorite sliced meat, cheese, and veggies.

Chapter Two

BEANS

Beans are the success story of the pressure cooker – their cooking time is cut to 1/3 or more, and they are delicious and tender. You can even pressure cook beans dry! Your pressure cooker's manual (or the cooking time chart on hipcooking.com) will tell you how long to pressure cook them. The recipes in this book use soaked beans – this ensures even cooking and even shorter pressure cooking time. When pressure cooking beans and recipes where beans are the main ingredient, never fill the pressure cooker to more than half-full and, unless otherwise indicated, use the Natural Release method.

Sage, Lentil & Sausage Risotto One Pot

Soaking lentils matches their cooking time to that of rice - giving you perfectly cooked lentils and al dente rice.

Stovetop Pressure Cook Time
7 minutes HIGH

Electric Pressure Cook Time
5 minutes HIGH

Serves
4

BEANS

INGREDIENTS

1 teaspoon olive oil
1 medium onion, chopped
8 ounces pork sausages
2 sprigs sage, torn (about 1 tablespoon dry)
1 cup Arborio rice
1 cup dry lentils, soaked overnight
3¼ cups vegetable stock

DIRECTIONS

1. In the pre-heated pressure cooker, add the olive oil, onion, sausage, and sage. Sauté until the sausage is browned (about 5 minutes).
2. Add the rice and mix until the rice is evenly coated with the sausage and onion mixture. Add the stock and strained lentils, mix well.
3. Close the lid and set the valve to the pressure position.

   Stovetop Pressure Cooker:
   Cook on HIGH for 7 minutes.

   Electric Pressure Cooker:
   Cook on HIGH for 5 minutes.

4. When time is up, release the pressure and open the lid. Mix well and serve immediately.

Recipe Tip:
You can use any kind of sausage for this recipe from chicken, to turkey and even tofu.

Smoky Red Bean & Turkey Chili

The turkey breast chunks fall apart into beautiful little meat shreds. Use this as a chili or to fill tacos, burritos or quesadillas.

Stovetop Pressure Cook Time
20 minutes HIGH

Electric Pressure Cook Time
25 minutes HIGH

Serves
6 - 8

INGREDIENTS

1 tablespoon olive oil
1½ - 2lb. turkey breast, sliced into 1" pieces
1 medium red onion, chopped
1 medium green bell pepper, chopped
1 teaspoon cumin seeds
½ teaspoon hot red pepper flakes
2 cups dry red kidney beans, soaked or quick-soaked
2 tablespoons tomato paste
1 cup chopped tomatoes
2 cups beef or chicken stock
1 tablespoon liquid smoke
Fresh coriander for garnish (optional)

DIRECTIONS

1. In the pre-heated cooker add oil and brown the turkey pieces on two sides - working in batches if needed (about 5 to 10 minutes). Remove the turkey pieces and set aside.
2. In the empty pressure cooker add the onion and green pepper. Sauté and occasionally stir until the onions have softened (about 3 minutes). Toss in the cumin and red pepper flakes and sauté for another 30 seconds.
3. Add the browned turkey, beans, tomato paste, chopped tomatoes, stock, and liquid smoke. Stir well. Close the lid and set the valve to the pressure position.

   Stovetop Pressure Cook Time:
   20 minutes HIGH

   Electric Pressure Cook Time:
   25 minutes HIGH

4. When time is up, release the pressure and open the cooker. Mix-in the cumin powder and simmer uncovered, occasionally stirring; until the desired consistency is reached (about 5 minutes).
5. While the contents are simmering, use a spoon/spatula to fish out the pieces of turkey and press them against the side of the cooker to break them up a little. Portion and sprinkle with garnish before serving.

Sweet Potatoes & Curried Black Eyed Peas One Pot

Slice the sweet potatoes in half to ensure they cook evenly (otherwise, the tips will cook much faster than the middle). If you substitute with white potatoes, you can leave them whole – don't forget to pierce the skin.

Stovetop & Electric Pressure Cook Time
12 minutes HIGH

Makes
2 cups

Accessories
Steamer basket & trivet

INGREDIENTS

3-4 medium sweet potatoes, sliced in half length-wise
6-8 tablespoons plain whole milk yogurt- or more to taste

For black-eyed peas:

1 tablespoon sesame oil
4 large garlic cloves, smashed
1 tablespoon ginger, finely sliced (or 1 teaspoon dried)
1 tablespoon Garam Masala
1 medium onion, chopped
1 cup black-eyed peas, rinsed
1 tablespoon tomato paste (double or triple concentrate)
1½ cups water
½ teaspoon sea salt
4½ ounces fresh spinach or baby spinach (about two cups)

DIRECTIONS

1. Pile the potatoes in the steamer basket (cut-face up, side-to-side) in crisscross layers and set aside.
2. In the pre-heated pressure cooker, add the sesame oil, ginger, garlic, and Garam Masala and sauté for about 30 seconds. Add the onion, black-eyed peas, tomato paste, and water.
3. Mix the contents well, place the trivet and steamer basket right on top of the black-eyed pea mixture.
4. Close the lid and set the valve to the pressure position.

   Stovetop & Electric Pressure Cook Time:
   12 minutes HIGH

5. When time is up, open the pressure cooker using the release method. Electric pressure cookers: Turn off the Keep Warm function and wait until the pressure indicator has gone down (about 20 to 30 minutes). Stovetop pressure cookers: Move the cooker off the burner and wait for the pressure to come down on its own (about 10 minutes).
6. Once the pressure is released, remove the steamer basket and divide the potato halves between dishes. Toss in the spinach and salt into the pressure cooker and mix enough to wilt using the residual heat of the beans.
7. Serve each potato half with a dollop of plain yogurt and a generous mound of black-eyed peas.

Boston "Baked" Beans

Did you know that both the maple syrup and the sugar count as part of the cooking liquid in this recipe? When they're heated, they turn into a liquid and help boil the beans to tender perfection. For a more traditional flavor, substitute the maple syrup with molasses. If you can't get your hands on Navy beans, replace with Great Northern or Cannellini without changing the cooking time.

Stovetop Pressure Cook Time
30 minutes HIGH

Electric Pressure Cook Time
35 minutes HIGH

Serves
6 - 8

INGREDIENTS

8 ounces bacon or pancetta, chopped
1 medium onion, chopped
4 tablespoons tomato paste
1 teaspoon allspice powder
½ teaspoon cinnamon powder
½ teaspoon cumin powder
2 cups water
½ cup maple syrup
⅓ cup raw sugar
1 bay leaf
2 cups dry Navy Beans soaked overnight
2 tablespoon Worcestershire sauce
1 teaspoon salt, or to taste

DIRECTIONS

1. Preheat the pressure cooker; add the bacon and sauté until it is crispy (about 5 minutes).
2. Remove the bacon, leaving most of the melted fat inside, and set aside. Add the onion and sauté in the bacon fat, lifting the brown bits on the base, until soft.
3. Mix in the tomato paste, allspice, cinnamon, cumin, and water. Then, add the sugar, maple syrup, bay leaf, and quick-soaked beans. Mix well.
4. Close the lid and set the valve to the pressure position.

   Stovetop Pressure Cook Time:
   30 minutes HIGH

   Electric Pressure Cook Time:
   35 minutes HIGH

5. When time is up, open the pressure cooker using the natural release method. Electric pressure cookers: Turn off the Keep Warm function mode and wait until the pressure indicator has gone down (about 20 to 30 minutes). Stovetop pressure cookers: Move the cooker off the burner and wait for the pressure to come down on its own (about 10 minutes).
6. Open the cooker and discard the bay leaf. Mix-in the Worcestershire sauce, salt, and reserved bacon bits. To thicken further, leave on simmer while mixing continuously.

Stewed Lentils with Potatoes and Spinach

The spinach gets tossed-in at the end and is flash-cooked in the heat of the lentils.

Stovetop & Electric Pressure Cook Time
10 minutes HIGH

Serves
4

INGREDIENTS

1 tablespoon olive oil
1 celery stalk, chopped
1 large onion, chopped
1 medium carrot, chopped
2 medium potatoes, diced skin-on
2 cups vegetable stock
1 bay leaf
1½ cups dry whole lentils, rinsed
1 teaspoon salt
2 cups fresh spinach leaves, washed
1 tablespoon fresh lemon juice

DIRECTIONS

1. In the pre-heated pressure cooker add the olive oil, celery, onion, carrot and sauté until the onion begins to soften (about 5 minutes). Add potatoes, stock, bay leaf, and lentils and mix well.
2. Close the lid and set the valve to the pressure position.

   Stovetop & Electric Pressure Cook Time:
   10 minutes HIGH

3. When time is up, open the pressure cooker with the Natural pressure release. Electric pressure cookers: Turn off the Keep Warm function and wait until the pressure indicator has gone down (about 20 to 30 minutes). Stovetop pressure cookers: Move the cooker off the burner and wait for the pressure to come down on its own (about 10 minutes).
4. When the pressure is released, open the lid and mix-in the salt and spinach leaves – fishing out the bay leaf when you find it – until the leaves are wilted. Squirt with lemon before serving.

Recipe Tip:
You can use any kind of whole lentil in this recipe without needing to adjust any of the other ingredients or cooking time.

Salsa Chickpeas with Brown Rice One Pot

The rice steams above the chickpeas that are boiling below – the extra tomatoes slow down the chickpea cooking time so they won't turn mushy in the time it takes to pressure cook the brown rice.

Stovetop Pressure Cook Time
18 minutes HIGH

Electric Pressure Cook Time
20 minutes HIGH

Serves
4

Accessories
Rack/trivet & 4-cup capacity heatproof bowl

INGREDIENTS

For Bain Marie Brown Rice:

1½ cups brown rice
2 cups water

For Salsa Chickpeas:

1 tablespoon olive oil
1 medium yellow onion, chopped
1 medium green bell pepper, chopped
1 teaspoon cumin powder
1 teaspoon dried oregano
¼ teaspoon red pepper flakes
1 (14 oz.) can chopped tomatoes
1 cup dry chickpeas, soaked overnight or quick-soaked
½ cup water
1 teaspoon salt
1 small red onion, finely chopped – for garnish

DIRECTIONS

1. In a 4-cup capacity heatproof container add the rice and water. If the container does not have a handle, construct an aluminum foil sling to lower and raise it out of the pressure cooker. Set aside.
2. In the pre-heated pressure cooker, add the oil, onions, bell pepper, cumin powder, oregano, and red pepper flakes. Sauté until the onion has softened.
3. Pour in the chopped tomatoes, chickpeas and water and mix well. Place the trivet/rack over the salsa chickpeas in the pressure cooker.
4. Lower the uncovered heat-proof container with the rice into the pressure cooker onto the trivet/rack basket. Close the lid and set the valve to the pressure position.

Stovetop Pressure Cook Time:
18 minutes HIGH

Electric Pressure Cook Time:
20 minutes HIGH

5. When time is up, open the pressure cooker using the natural release method. Electric pressure cookers: Turn off the Keep Warm function and wait until the pressure indicator has gone down (about 20 to 30 minutes). Stovetop pressure cookers: Move the cooker off the burner and wait for the pressure to come down on its own (about 10 minutes).
6. After all the pressure is released, carefully lift out the heat-proof container and fluff the rice. Serve on individual dishes.
7. Mix in the salt into the salsa chickpeas, spoon it out and serve with a sprinkling of raw red onion.

Easy Hummus

BEANS

We pressure cook the chickpeas a little longer than their recommended pressure cooking time to ensure they are fully cooked and ready to melt into a creamy spread.

Stovetop Pressure Cook Time
15 minutes HIGH

Electric Pressure Cook Time
18 minutes HIGH

Serves
4

INGREDIENTS

1 cup dry chickpeas, soaked or quick-soaked
4 cups water
1 bay leaf
3-4 garlic cloves, finely chopped
2 tablespoons tahini
½ teaspoon sea salt, or to taste
1 lemon, juiced
¼ teaspoon cumin powder
½ bunch parsley, chopped (about ¼ cup of leaves)
¼ teaspoon paprika
2 tablespoons extra virgin olive oil

DIRECTIONS

1. Rinse the chickpeas and put them in your pressure cooker with the water and bay leaf. Close the lid and set the valve to the pressure position.

   Stovetop Pressure Cook Time:
   15 minutes HIGH

   Electric Pressure Cook Time:
   18 minutes HIGH

2. When time is up, open the pressure cooker using the natural release method. Electric pressure cookers: Turn off the Keep Warm function and wait until the pressure indicator has gone down (about 20 to 30 minutes). Stovetop pressure cookers: Move the cooker off the burner and wait for the pressure to come down on its own (about 10 minutes).
3. Once all the pressure is released, drain the chickpeas, reserving all of the cooking liquid - you will need some of this to add back when pureeing the chickpeas.
4. Optionally pull out some whole chickpeas to reserve for the garnish and then pour chickpeas into a food processor, or puree with a stick blender or potato masher.
5. Add the garlic, tahini and ½ a cup of cooking liquid into a food processor or the cooker if using a stick blender/potato masher. Puree the mixture to your liking, slowly adding back enough cooking liquid to get to the right consistency (generally about a cup total).
6. When the hummus has reached the right consistency, add the lemon and salt and mix well. Transfer the mixture into a communal dipping bowl, drizzle with olive oil. Sprinkle with paprika and fresh parsley, and a few whole cooked chickpeas (if using) and serve.

Split Pea & Prosciutto Soup

You can replace the prosciutto with bacon or a cooked ham-hock. If using a ham-hock strip off the meat and reserve, only tossing the bone with scraps into the soup for the pressure cooking step. Split peas are notorious for gumming-up pressure cooker release valves – so make sure to follow the directions in the recipe for using the Natural Release method.

Stovetop & Electric Pressure Cook Time
5 minutes HIGH

Serves
4 - 6

BEANS

INGREDIENTS

1 tablespoon olive oil
3½ ounces prosciutto, sliced into strips
1 medium white or yellow onion, diced
1 celery stalk, diced
1 carrot, large diced
2 cups dried green split peas, rinsed
6 cups water
1" strip of Kombu
1 teaspoon sea salt

DIRECTIONS

1. Add the oil and prosciutto into the pressure cooker, then brown until the prosciutto becomes crispy. Remove most of it from the pressure cooker and set aside – leaving the oil and rendered fat in the pressure cooker.
2. Add the onion, celery, and carrot to the pressure cooker and sauté in the fat until the onions have softened (about 5 minutes) - use the wetness of the veggies to lift the brown fond that will have formed on the base.
3. Add the split peas, water, Kombu, and salt. Mix well and make sure that the pressure cooker is no more than ½ full. Close the lid and set the valve to the pressure position.

   Stovetop & Electric Pressure Cook Time:
   5 minutes HIGH

4. When time is up, open the pressure cooker using the natural release method. Electric pressure cookers: Turn off the Keep Warm function and wait until the pressure indicator has gone down (about 20 to 30 minutes). Stovetop pressure cookers: Move the cooker off the burner and wait for the pressure to come down on its own (about 10 minutes).
5. Crumble most of the prosciutto into the soup (reserve a few strips for garnish), remove the Kombu, and serve the soup with a crunch strip of prosciutto as garnish.

Max
2/3

Chapter Three

RICE & GRAINS

Rice and grains are a little tricky to pressure cook – that's because there is almost no evaporation in the pressure cooker. That means that both the grains and the cooking liquid need to be measured carefully! Remember, any ingredient you add will also add liquid to the recipe – follow the instructions in the recipe to successfully create your rice and grain dishes.

New Orleans Dirty Rice

The "dirty" part of this recipe is liver! It crumbles into little pieces. If liver is not to your family's taste, substitute it with the same amount of sausage (so, instead of using just 6 ounces of sausage, up the recipe to 14 ounces).

Stovetop & Electric Pressure Cook Time
3 minutes HIGH

Serves
4 - 6

INGREDIENTS

1 tablespoon olive oil
1 medium onion, chopped
1 medium green pepper, chopped
8 ounces chicken livers, chopped to ¼"
6 ounces Andouille sausage
(or 3 ounces chopped bacon and 3 ounces of spicy salami)
2 stalks celery, chopped
2 garlic cloves, minced
2 teaspoons creole seasoning
2 cups long-grain rice (like Basmati)
2½ cups vegetable stock (or water)

RICE & GRAINS

DIRECTIONS

1. In the pre-heated pressure cooker add the oil, onion, bell pepper and sauté until the onion is just starting to soften.
2. Push the onion aside and add the raw liver, moving it around until most of it has turned pink.
3. Add the sausage and celery and sauté everything together, occasionally stirring, for about 3 more minutes.
4. Add the garlic, creole seasoning and rice and mix everything together well. Pour in the stock; quickly scrape the bottom of the cooker using the stock to lift up any bits that may have stuck themselves to the base of the cooker.
5. Close the lid and set the valve to the pressure position.

   Stovetop & Electric Pressure Cook Time:
   3 minutes HIGH

6. When time is up, open the pressure cooker using the natural release method. Electric pressure cookers: Turn off the Keep Warm function and wait until the pressure indicator has gone down (about 20 to 30 minutes). Stovetop pressure cookers: Move the cooker off the burner and wait for the pressure to come down on its own (about 10 minutes).
7. Serve with a sprinkling of fresh parsley and a bottle of Tabasco sauce.

Confetti Basmati Rice

This is a lovely side dish that includes a sprinkling of colorful vegetables that make this dish as pretty as it is tasty.

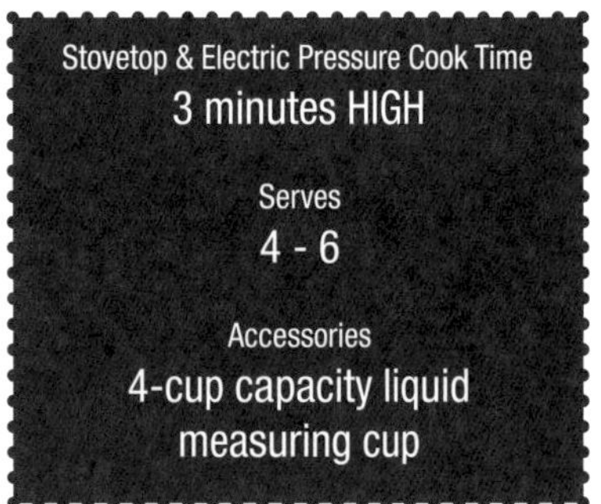

INGREDIENTS

1 tablespoon olive oil
1 medium onion, chopped
1 medium bell pepper (any color)
1 carrot, grated
water as needed
2 cups Basmati or long-grain rice
½ cup peas (fresh or frozen)
1 teaspoon salt

DIRECTIONS

1. In the heated pressure cooker, swirl in the olive oil and onion and sauté until translucent.
2. In the meantime, in a 4-cup capacity liquid measuring cup, add the bell pepper, grated carrots and pat down lightly into an even layer.
3. Pour water into the measuring cup with the veggies until you reach the 3 cup mark and set aside. Back to the pressure cooker, pour in the rice, peas, and salt. Mix well.
4. Now, add the water and veggies into the pressure cooker. Mix well. Close the lid and set the valve to the pressure position.

   Stovetop & Electric Pressure Cook Time:
   3 minutes HIGH

5. When time is up, open the pressure cooker using the natural release method. Electric pressure cookers: Turn off the Keep Warm function and wait until the pressure indicator has gone down (about 20 to 30 minutes). Stovetop pressure cookers: Move the cooker off the burner and wait for the pressure to come down on its own (about 10 minutes).
6. Fluff the rice with a fork, and serve!

Recipe Tip:
The trick to adding vegetables to the rice in this recipe is to measure some of them as cooking liquid.

Hot Tamales with Your Fave Filling

Fill hot tamales with your favorite filling; pre-cooked shredded pork, black beans or veggies.

Stovetop Pressure Cook Time
15 minutes HIGH

Electric Pressure Cook Time
20 minutes HIGH

Makes
36-40 depending on size

Accessories
Steamer basket & trivet

INGREDIENTS

1 pack corn husks
2-3 cups of Carnitas meat or your favorite filling
4 cups prepared Masa Harina

DIRECTIONS

1. Rinse the corn husks and put them in a large shallow dish, like a casserole, and add enough boiling water to cover them.
2. Use a heavy object, like a heavy lid from a pan, to keep the husks immersed. Just before starting to construct the tamales, flip the corn husks around so the ones that were soaking on the bottom are now on the top.
3. Lay out one or three corn husks and wipe them down with a kitchen towel to dry, and then spread an even layer of masa in the middle top of the husk. Place a small amount of meat (or filling of your choice) in the middle and wet it with carnitas cooking liquid or chili sauce.
4. Carefully fold the sides closed, and then fold the bottom part upwards - without squeezing - leaving the tops open.
5. Add 2 cups of water to the pressure cooker, add the trivet and steamer basket, and place the tamales in the basket open-side up. It may take a bit of arranging and some may be diagonal but no horizontal tamales! Cook in two batches if necessary.
6. Close the lid and set the valve to the pressure position.

   Stovetop Pressure Cook Time:
   15 minutes HIGH

   Electric Pressure Cook Time:
   20 minutes HIGH

7. When time is up, open the pressure cooker using the natural release method. Electric pressure cookers: Turn off the Keep Warm function and wait until the pressure indicator has gone down (about 20 to 30 minutes). Stovetop pressure cookers: Move the cooker off the burner and wait for the pressure to come down on its own (about 10 minutes).
8. Serve hot tamales in their wrappers.

Recipe Tip:
If you only have a few tamales, tie them together in groups of three with kitchen string so that they can stand up on their own in the steamer basket.

Spanish Rice

Even though this recipe is called "Spanish Rice," it is actually native to Mexico but is more commonly known as "Arroz Rojo" or Red Rice.

Stovetop & Electric Pressure Cook Time
5 minutes HIGH

Serves
4 - 6

INGREDIENTS

1 tablespoon vegetable oil
1 onion, chopped
2 cups medium or long-,grain white rice
1 cup chopped tomatoes and their juice or canned chopped tomatoes
2½ cups water
2 teaspoons salt
⅛ teaspoon cayenne pepper
1 teaspoon oregano
1 green onion, chopped (optional)

DIRECTIONS

1. In the pressure cooker, add the vegetable oil and onion and sauté until the onions begin to soften (about 5 minutes).
2. Add the rice and sauté until the first few grains begin to brown (about 3 minutes). Add the tomatoes, water, salt, oregano, and cayenne pepper, mix well and be sure to scrape the bottom of the pan well to un-stick any rice.
3. Close the lid and set the valve to the pressure position.

   Stovetop & Electric Pressure Cook Time:
   5 minutes HIGH
4. When the time is done, release pressure and open the lid. Mix the rice, and serve with finely chopped green onion garnish.

Recipe Tip:
This is the tomato-y rice that can be used as a filling for burritos!

Steamed Savory Quick-Bread

This recipe will make a moist loaf of bread – it's particularly useful for cooks on the go in their RV's, living on boats or any other limited space where turning on the oven to bake is not possible, but there is still a yearning for fresh home-made bread.

Stovetop Pressure Cook Time
20 minutes HIGH

Electric Pressure Cook Time
25 minutes HIGH

Yeilds
1 small loaf

Accessories
heat-proof container (preferably cylindrical)

INGREDIENTS

1 teaspoon olive oil
2 cups all-purpose flour
½ teaspoon bicarbonate baking soda (not baking powder!)
1 teaspoon salt
1¼ cup whole milk plain yogurt (or sour milk, or milk with 1¼ tablespoons of vinegar)
Water as needed

DIRECTIONS

1. Oil a heat-proof 4 cup capacity container with a teaspoon of olive oil.
2. In a medium mixing bowl, add flour, baking soda, and salt. Stir everything together with a fork and then add the yogurt.
3. Stir lightly to incorporate, and then gently knead. The mixture should be a bit chunky and flaky - break up the biggest flakes and combine back into the mixture for about a minute.
4. Gather the dough together and see if it will hold together into a ball - it will be a little bit sticky. If it doesn't stay into a ball, sprinkle a little water. Knead gently for about a minute to amalgamate everything.

Recipe Tip:
This is a take on the "coffee can" bread that doesn't necessarily need to be made in a coffee can. Use any heat-proof cylindrical container that will fit in your pressure cooker.

5. Elongate the mixture and lower it in the oiled container, adding a little splash of oil on top of the bread. Cover with foil and, to ensure room for expansion, make a small pleat in the middle of the foil.
   Tie a string around the edge to keep the container tightly closed (do not use plastic, glass or hermetic lids).
6. Lower the container into the cooker base and pour in hot water from the tap to half the height of the cylindrical container. Close the lid and set the valve to the pressure position.

   Stovetop Pressure Cook Time:
   20 minutes HIGH

   Electric Pressure Cook Time:
   25 minutes HIGH

   NOTE: Cooking times may vary depending on the width and materials of the container used (glass and ceramic will take longer than stainless steel or aluminum).

7. When time is up, open the pressure cooker using the natural release method. Electric pressure cookers: Turn off the Keep Warm function and wait until the pressure indicator has gone down (about 20 to 30 minutes). Stovetop pressure cookers: Move the cooker off the burner and wait for the pressure to come down on its own (about 10 minutes).
8. Carefully lift the container out of the pressure cooker and remove the foil lid. Unmold the loaf and put on a cooling rack to rest for 10 minutes before slicing.
9. Slice and serve warm with fresh butter.

Porcini Mushroom & Red Wine Risotto

The magic ratio here is 1 cup rice to 2 cups broth or ½ cup rice to 1 cup broth - which is handy to know, because this is the amount you will need per serving in case you need increase or decrease the recipe.

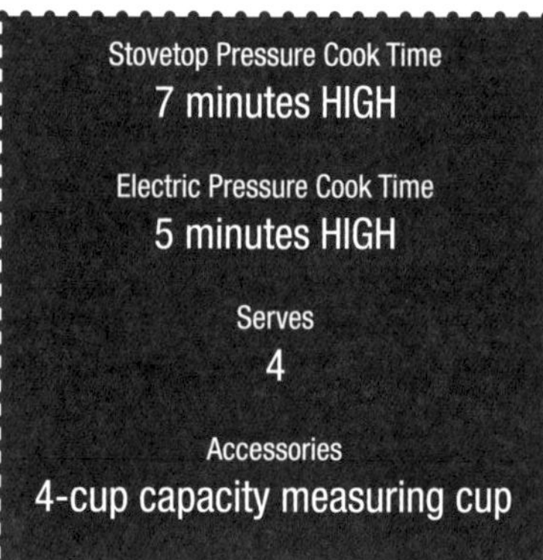

INGREDIENTS:

1 ounce dried porcini mushrooms
2 cups water
1 tablespoon olive oil
1 medium red onion
¼ cup tarty red wine like Merlot or Chianti
2 cups of Arborio Rice (can be substituted with "Short Grain White Pearl" rice)
2 cups chicken or vegetable stock
1 teaspoon salt
1 tablespoon butter
1 sprig fresh thyme

Recipe Tip:
Sometimes recipes like risotto can benefit from additional cooking time. If you feel your recipe could use more time to cook, use the natural release method instead.

DIRECTIONS

1. In a heat-proof 4-cup measuring cup add the dried porcini mushrooms and 2 cups of hot water. Cover tightly and set aside.
2. In the pressure cooker on medium heat add the oil and onion. Sauté the onion until it becomes translucent (about 5 minutes).
3. Add the rice and lightly toast it to release the starch. When the rice is thoroughly mixed with the onion and oil, pour in the wine to un-stick any grains from the bottom of the cooker and stir until all of the liquid has evaporated.
4. Add the porcini mushrooms and their soaking liquid, stock, and salt, mix well. Close the lid and set the valve to the pressure position.

Stovetop Pressure Cook Time:	**Electric Pressure Cook Time:**
7 minutes HIGH	5 minutes HIGH

5. When time is up, release pressure and remove the lid. The risotto should appear just slightly too wet – this is OK. Stir the rice, and it will continue to absorb the extra liquid in about 30 seconds.
6. Mix-in the butter and sprinkle with fresh thyme before serving.

Chapter Four

PASTA

These recipes give a general pressure cooking time – but in Italy, every pasta shape has its own cooking time. If you're using a different type of pasta from the one specified in the recipe you can adjust the cooking time by halving the recommended cooking time on the package – and then cooking at low pressure as indicated in the recipe.

Fusilli with Tuna & Black Olives

This delicious dish can be served hot or cold, making it perfect for any season.

Stovetop & Electric Pressure Cook Time
3 minutes LOW

Serves
4 - 6

INGREDIENTS

1 tablespoon olive oil
1 garlic clove
3 anchovies
2 cups tomato puree
1½ teaspoons salt
16 ounces fusilli pasta – or another short pasta shape
2 (5½ ounce) cans tuna packed in olive oil
3-4 cups water - to cover
½ cup black pitted olives

DIRECTIONS

1. In the cooker on medium heat add the oil, garlic, and anchovies. Sauté until the anchovies begin to disintegrate, and the garlic cloves just start to turn golden.
2. Add the tomato puree and salt and mix together. Pour in the uncooked pasta, and the contents of one tuna can, mixing to coat the dry pasta evenly.
3. Flatten the pasta in an even layer and pour in just enough water to cover. Close the lid and set the valve to the pressure position.

   Stovetop & Electric Pressure Cook Time:
   3 minutes LOW

4. When time is up, release the pressure and open the cooker. Mix in the last can of tuna and sprinkle with olives before serving.

PASTA

Recipe Tip:
You can make this recipe with whole-wheat or gluten-free pasta without changing the quantities or cooking time.

Spicy Penne

Don't substitute pasta sauce from a jar – it contains thickeners, starches, and gums that will prevent the pressure cooker from reaching pressure.

Stovetop & Electric Pressure Cook Time
5 minutes LOW

Serves
4 - 6

INGREDIENTS

1 tablespoon olive oil
2-3 garlic cloves, smashed
2 fresh hot chili peppers, chopped (or 1 tsp. of hot pepper flakes)
1 pinch dry oregano
1 (14½ ounce) Penne pasta
14½ ounce can (or 2 cups) tomato puree
1 teaspoon salt
3-4 cups water - to cover
Extra virgin olive oil for garnish

DIRECTIONS

1. In the cooker, on low heat, add a swirl of olive oil, the garlic cloves, hot peppers/flakes and oregano (grinding it between your fingers as you sprinkle it in).
2. Allow the ingredients to infuse the oil until the cloves begin to sizzle and turn lightly golden. Pour in the pasta, the tomato puree, salt and just enough water to cover the pasta.
3. Stir everything together and flatten the pasta out in an even layer with your wooden spoon, or spatula – it's ok if a few points stick out here and there. Close the lid and set the valve to the pressure position.

   Stovetop & Electric Pressure Cook Time:
   5 minutes LOW

4. When time is up, release the pressure and open the cooker. Give the contents a stir and let the pasta sit for about a minute before serving.
5. Top each bowl with a small swirl of fresh extra virgin olive oil.

PASTA

Recipe Tip:
This is a very simple recipe that highlights great ingredients – use the highest quality tomato purée you can find.

Bowties with Broccoli & Sausage

In this recipe, the broccoli florets steam above the pasta so it does not become overcooked. Then, before serving everything is mixed together which breaks-up the broccoli and distributes it evenly through the dish.

Stovetop & Electric Pressure Cook Time
5 minutes LOW

Serves
4 - 6

INGREDIENTS

1 tablespoon olive oil
1 pound sausage - your favorite kind
1 pound bowtie pasta
1 tablespoon tomato paste concentrate
1 teaspoon salt
3-4 cups water - to cover
8-12 ounces broccoli florets
2 garlic cloves, finely minced

DIRECTIONS

1. Add the oil to the cooker and then squeeze the sausage meat of out its casing into the pressure cooker. Break-up the sausage and sauté occasionally stirring until crispy and golden (about 5 minutes).
2. Once the sausage is crispy and fully cooked, lift it out of the pressure cooker and set aside. You can also remove some of the fat at this point if you prefer.
3. Add a small splash of water and lift-up the browned bits stuck to the base of the pressure cooker. Next add the pasta, tomato paste, and salt. Mix the ingredients inside the pressure cooker well.
4. Smooth out the top of the pasta into a somewhat flat layer, and add just enough water to cover the pasta – it's ok if a few points stick out here and there.
5. On top of the pasta mixture, add the broccoli florets - stem-side down. Close the lid and set the valve to the pressure position.

   Stovetop & Electric Pressure Cook Time:
   5 minutes LOW

6. When time is up, release the pressure and open the cooker. Mix-in the garlic, break-up the broccoli, and add the fried sausage pieces back into the cooker and serve.

Macaroni and Ricotta Cheese

This is a simple recipe, which basically shows how you can cook pasta by itself in a pressure cooker and then mix-in your favorite sauce. Ricotta is one option, and so are other pasta sauces that shouldn't be cooked such as basil or sun-dried tomato pesto.

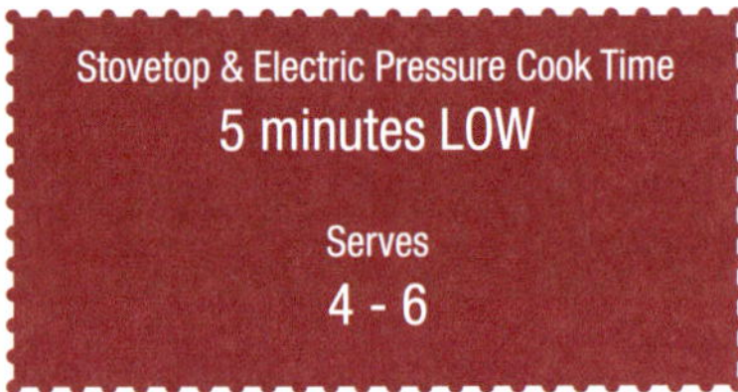

INGREDIENTS

16 ounces pipes, elbow macaroni, penne
or short tubular Pasta that can scoop up the cream sauce
1 tablespoon Olive Oil
1 teaspoon sea salt
3-4 cups water - to cover
8 ounces sheep or cow milk ricotta
1 sprig fresh basil
1 teaspoon black pepper, freshly ground
½ cup Pecorino Romano cheese, grated

DIRECTIONS

1. In the cooker, add a swirl of olive oil, pasta, salt, and enough water to just cover the pasta. Smooth the pasta out with a spatula to get an even layer and submerge as much pasta in as little water as possible.
2. Close the lid and set the valve to the pressure position.

   Stovetop & Electric Pressure Cook Time:
   5 minutes LOW

3. When time is up, release the pressure and open the cooker. Pour out half of the cooking water from the pressure cooker into the sink – leave the rest in to soften the ricotta cheese (drain completely if making plain pasta).
4. Mix in the ricotta cheese and top each serving with Pecorino Romano cheese, pepper, and torn basil leaves. Serve immediately.

Chapter Five

FISH & SEAFOOD

Seafood is extremely delicate and prone to over-cooking. That's why these recipes use "low" pressure. Low pressure also means the food is pressure cooked at a lower temperature, which ensures your dinner will not be overcooked!

Steamed Mediterranean Style Fish

FISH & SEAFOOD

This is a great recipe to use with any white fish filet. Fish is generally very delicate so the use low pressure, the protection of the heat-proof dish and cherry tomatoes ensure that the fish is not overcooked.

Stovetop Pressure Cook Time
7 minutes LOW

Electric Pressure Cook Time
8 minutes LOW

Serves
4

Accessories
Rack/trivet & 4-cup capacity heatproof bowl

INGREDIENTS

3 fish fillets, any kind of white fish
1 cup water
1 pound Cherry tomatoes=, halved
1 cup black salt-cured olives (Taggiesche, French or Kalamata)
2 tablespoons pickled capers
1 bunch of fresh thyme
Olive oil
1 clove of garlic, pressed
½ teaspoon salt, or to taste
¼ teaspoon pepper, or to taste

DIRECTIONS

1. Add the water and steamer basket to the base of the cooker.
2. Line the bottom of the heat-proof bowl with cherry tomato halves, add Thyme (reserve a few springs for garnish).
3. Place the fish fillets over the cherry tomatoes, sprinkle with remaining tomatoes, crushed garlic, a dash of olive oil and a pinch of salt.
4. Lower the heatproof bowl into the pressure cooker on top of the trivet/rack - if your heat proof dish does not have handles construct them by making a long aluminum sling.
5. Close the lid and set the valve to the pressure position.

   Stovetop Pressure Cook Time:
   7 minutes LOW

   Electric Pressure Cook Time:
   8 minutes LOW

6. When time is up, release the pressure and open the lid.
7. Distribute fish into individual plates, top with cherry tomatoes, and sprinkle with olives, capers, fresh thyme, a crackle of pepper and a little swirl of olive oil before serving.

Recipe Tip:
Lining the heatproof bowl with cherry tomatoes will keep the fish fillets from sticking to it.

Steamed Mussels

FISH & SEAFOOD

Using the pressure cooker assures that every single mussel opens at the same time. Make it spicy by adding a teaspoon of hot pepper flakes in the steaming liquid (this won't make them spicy during cooking, but it well when you pour the spicy steaming liquid on top before serving).

Stovetop Pressure Cook Time
1 minutes LOW

Electric Pressure Cook Time
2 minutes LOW

Serves
4 - 6

Accessories
Steamer basket & trivet

INGREDIENTS

2 pounds fresh mussels, cleaned and de-bearded
1 tablespoon olive oil
1 clove garlic, smashed
¼ cup of dry white wine, such as chardonnay
½ cup water
1 bunch fresh parsley, chopped

DIRECTIONS

To clean the mussels: Right before cooking, hold the mussel with the round end towards you and pull on the little "beard" sliding it in the opening toward you as you pull. Then, clean the shells by scrubbing with a nylon brush or scrubby sponge (with no detergent residue).

1. Arrange the mussels in the steamer basket and set aside.
2. In the pre-heated pressure cooker, add a swirl of olive oil and garlic and sauté for 30 seconds. Pour in the wine, and then the water.
3. Quickly lower down the trivet and steamer basket with the mussels. Close the lid and set the valve to the pressure position.

   Stovetop Pressure Cook Time:
   1 minute LOW

   Electric Pressure Cook Time:
   2 minutes LOW

4. When time is up, release the pressure and open the cooker.
5. Place the mussels in individual appetizer plates, scoop the steaming liquid with garlic and wine over them and sprinkle with parsley.

Recipe Tip:
This recipe has no salt because the mussels open during cooking and release the salty sea water into the steaming liquid below.

Swordfish Teriyaki

FISH & SEAFOOD

The teriyaki marinade creates a flavorful, light, and cholesterol-free meal.

Stovetop Pressure Cook Time
2 minutes HIGH

Electric Pressure Cook Time
3 minutes HIGH

Serves
4

INGREDIENTS

1½ - 1¾ pounds swordfish or tuna steaks cut in 1½"cubes
2 red peppers cut in 1½" pieces
10 scallions, in 1½" lengths, thicker portions only
2 tablespoons oil

TERIYAKI SAUCE

½ cup soy sauce
2 tablespoons sugar
2 tablespoons dry sherry
1 tablespoon rice wine or other white wine
1½ teaspoons grated fresh ginger
2 cloves garlic, minced
1 tablespoon sesame oil
1 teaspoon hoisin sauce

DIRECTIONS

1. In a bowl large enough to hold the fish, mix the Teriyaki Sauce ingredients. Add the fish, peppers, and scallions to half of the marinade and refrigerate for 30 minutes. Remove from the marinade and drain well.
2. Sauté the scallions and peppers in 2 tablespoons of oil until crispy and tender about 5 minutes. Remove to a platter and keep warm.
3. Add the fish to the cooker and sear on all sides.
4. Add the reserved vegetables and marinade to the cooker. Close the lid and set the valve to the pressure position.

   Stovetop Pressure Cook Time:
   2 minutes HIGH

   Electric Pressure Cook Time:
   3 minutes HIGH

5. When time is up, release the pressure and open the cooker. Serve immediately.

Bouillabaisse

An effortless dish, outstanding for entertaining company and sure to please the seafood enthusiast in your life.

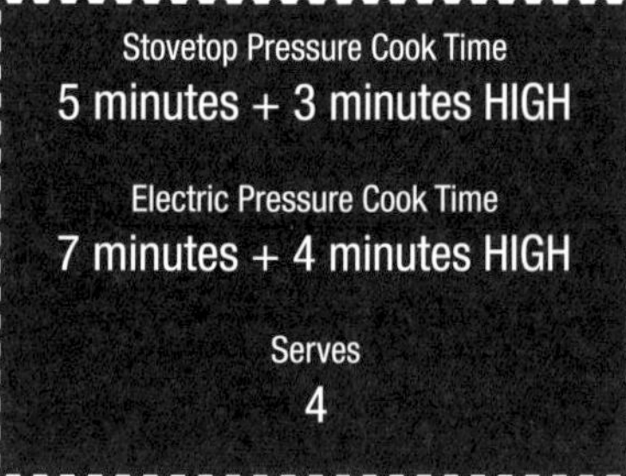

INGREDIENTS

1 pound hearty fish filets cut into chunks
1 pound lobster tail, cut into chunks
12 ounces Scallops
¼ pound shrimp
6 clams in shells
4 cups water
3 tablespoons olive oil
2 onions, chopped
2 cloves garlic
2 tablespoons parsley, chopped
1 bay leaf
1 teaspoon thyme
¼ teaspoon saffron (optional)
Salt and pepper to taste

DIRECTIONS

1. Sauté the onions in the cooker, about 3 minutes.
2. Add the garlic, parsley, tomatoes, bay leaf, thyme, optional saffron, water, salt, and pepper. Close the lid and set the valve to the pressure position.

   Stovetop Pressure Cook Time: 5 minutes HIGH
   Electric Pressure Cook Time: 7 minutes HIGH

3. When time is up, release the pressure and open the lid.
4. Add the fish and seafood and stir well. Close the lid and set the valve to the pressure position.

   Stovetop Pressure Cook Time: 3 minutes HIGH
   Electric Pressure Cook Time: 4 minutes HIGH

5. When time is up, release the pressure and open the lid. Remove the bay leaf and serve hot.

Piquant Shrimp

Just a little spicy because who doesn't love a little kick.

Stovetop Pressure Cook Time
4 minutes + 1 minute HIGH

Electric Pressure Cook Time
5 minutes + 1 minutes HIGH

Serves
4

INGREDIENTS

2 tablespoons olive oil
1½ pounds large shrimp d shelled
1 cup minced onion
2 tablespoons minced parsley
4 cloves garlic d minced
2 teaspoons paprika
¼ cup dry white wine
½ cup fish stock or clam juice
1 cup tomato sauce
Pinch of sugar
Pinch of saffron
1 teaspoon crushed hot red pepper
1 bay leaf
¼ teaspoon thyme
Salt, freshly ground pepper to taste

DIRECTIONS

1. Sauté the shrimp in olive oil in the cooker. Remove the shrimp to a platter.
2. Add the onion to the cooker (add a bit more oil if necessary) and sauté until wilted.
3. Stir in the parsley, garlic, paprika, and wine. Boil and reduce by half.
4. Add the fish stock, tomato sauce, sugar, saffron, hot red pepper flakes, bay leaf, thyme, salt, and pepper.
5. Close the lid and set the valve to the pressure position.

   Stovetop Pressure Cook Time:
   4 minutes HIGH

   Electric Pressure Cook Time:
   5 minutes HIGH

6. When time is up, release the pressure and open the cooker. If the sauce is too thin, boil it down a bit.
7. Add the shrimp, close the lid, and set the valve to the pressure position.

   Stovetop & Electric Pressure Cook Time:
   1 minute HIGH

8. When done, release the pressure and open the cooker. Discard the bay leaf. Serve over rice.

Salmon with Spinach and Lemon Sauce

FISH & SEAFOOD

Just a little spicy because who doesn't love a little kick.

Stovetop Pressure Cook Time
3 minutes + 3 minute HIGH

Electric Pressure Cook Time
3 minutes + 7 minutes HIGH

Serves
6

INGREDIENTS

1½ teaspoons salt, divided
20 ounces of fresh spinach leaves, cleaned and rinsed
2 tablespoons olive oil
1 medium onion, cut in half and sliced
2 garlic cloves, minced
2 tablespoons minced fresh broadleaf parsley
1 cup bottles clam juice
¼ cup fresh lemon juice
¼ teaspoon white pepper
1½ teaspoons dried crumbled dill
4 (6-8 oz.) salmon steaks at least 1-inch thick
1 teaspoon corn starch dissolved in 1 tablespoon of cold water
2 large egg yolks
Zest of a lemon

DIRECTIONS

1. Place one cup water, 1 teaspoon of salt and the spinach leaves in the cooker. Close the lid and set the valve to the pressure position.

   Stovetop & Electric Pressure Cook Time:
   3 minutes High

2. Remove the spinach from the cooker, drain thoroughly and place on a platter. Cover and keep warm in a low-temperature oven. Dry the cooker with a paper towel.
3. Sauté the onions, garlic and parsley for about 2 minutes. Stir in the clam juice, lemon juice, remaining salt, pepper, and dill.
4. Add salt, pepper, and lemon zest to the salmon. Place the salmon in the cooker in a single layer. Close the lid and set the valve to the pressure position.

   Stovetop Pressure Cook Time:
   3 minutes HIGH

   Electric Pressure Cook Time:
   7 minutes HIGH

5. When done, release the pressure and open the cooker.
6. Using a slotted spatula, transfer the salmon to the warmed platter and cover to keep warm. Pour off all but 1/3 cup of the cooking liquid in the cooker and warm the liquid.
7. Stir in the egg yolks and cornstarch mixture. Stir until it begins to thicken.
8. To serve, arrange a portion of spinach on each plate. Top each with a salmon steak and spoon sauce over the salmon. Garnish with sprigs of fresh parsley or thin lemon slices.

Chapter Six

MEAT

Meat is quickly tenderized in the pressure cooker in a short time – in fact, the biggest mistake most cooks make when starting out is over-cooking the meat. Be sure to follow the cooking times recommended in these recipes. Then, check the meat. If it is not entirely cooked, you just need to close the pressure cooker and go for a few more minutes (it will take much less time to reach pressure the second time around) – but usually, it will be perfectly cooked.

Pork Chops with Fennel Seeds and Apples

The pressure cooker turns the apples into a delicious sauce – for the pork chops.

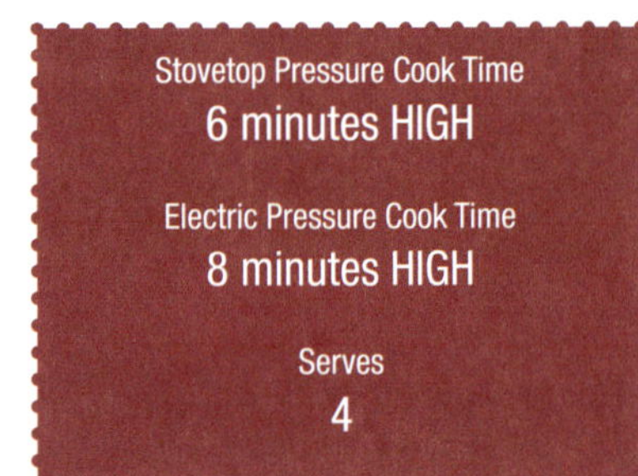

INGREDIENTS

4 thick-cut pork chops (about ¾")
1 teaspoon fennel seeds
1 teaspoon salt
1 teaspoon pepper
3 apples (any kind), sliced and cored
1 tablespoon vegetable oil
¾ cup meat stock

MEAT

DIRECTIONS

1. Sprinkle the pork chops with fennel, salt, and pepper. In the cooker, add the oil and brown all of the chops on one side only - only two at a time may fit depending on the size of the pressure cooker base, or the chops so work in batches.
2. When all of the chops have been browned and set aside, add the apple slices into the empty cooker. Arrange the pork chops brown-side up on top of the apples, overlapping as needed.
3. Pour any juice from the chops and meat stock around the edges of the chops. Close the lid and set the valve to the pressure position.

   Stovetop Pressure Cook Time:
   6 minutes HIGH

   Electric Pressure Cook Time:
   8 minutes HIGH

4. When time is up, release the pressure and open the cooker. Lift the pork chops out of the cooker and immediately smother in the apple sauce.

Recipe Tip:
Smothering the chops in the apple sauce will keep the juice from the chops from evaporating and losing flavor.

Easy BBQ Pork Ribs

Although most things come out of the pressure cooker looking just "boiled" this recipe gets its just-off-the-grill scorch from a little broiling at the end of the recipe.

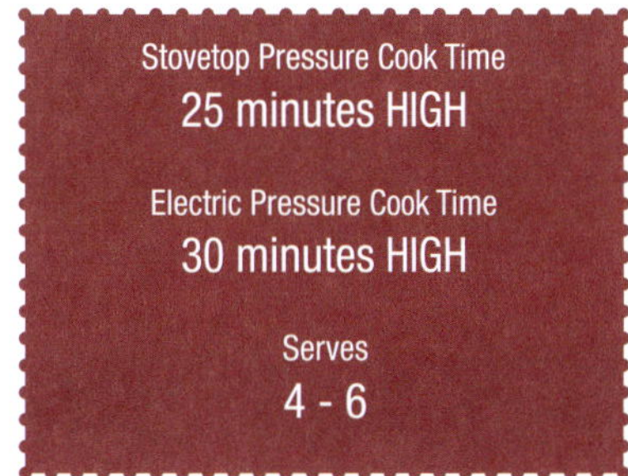

INGREDIENTS

1 cup water
2 racks baby back pork
2 cups prepared barbecue sauce

DIRECTIONS

1. Add the water to the cooker base.
2. Coat the pork rib racks with half of the BBQ sauce (1 cup) and place the rack in the cooker standing-up vertically – make sure not to crowd the ribs, leaving space around each rack for the steam to cook the meat.
3. Close the lid and set the valve to the pressure position.

   Stovetop Pressure Cook Time:
   25 minutes HIGH

   Electric Pressure Cook Time:
   30 minutes HIGH

4. When time is up, open the pressure cooker using the natural release method. Electric pressure cookers: Turn off the Keep Warm function and wait until the pressure indicator has gone down (about 20 to 30 minutes). Stovetop pressure cookers: Move the cooker off the burner and wait for the pressure to come down on its own (about 10 minutes).
5. Carefully remove the ribs and arrange flat on an oven pan. Spread the remaining BBQ sauce on the ribs and slide under the broiler until the ribs are slightly singed (about 5 minutes).

Recipe Tip:
Try this recipe with any flavor BBQ sauce for added variety.

Meatballs in Tomato Sauce

Stovetop Pressure Cook Time
5 minutes HIGH

Serves
4 - 6

Play around with the ingredients for different flavors - use seasoned instead of plain breadcrumbs, use another kind of hard cheese (halve the salt if using pecorino) or replace the oregano with hot pepper flakes for a spicy touch.

INGREDIENTS

For the meatballs:

1 medium onion, finely chopped and divided
½ cup plain dried bread crumbs
⅓ cup grated parmesan cheese
½ teaspoon dried oregano
¼ teaspoon black pepper
2 teaspoons salt, divided
½ cup whole milk
1 pound mixed ground meat
(for example pork, beef, and veal or just beef)
1 large egg, lightly beaten

For the sauce:

1 tablespoon olive oil
1 medium carrot, finely chopped
½ celery stalk, finely chopped
2¾ cups chopped tomatoes
1 cup water

Recipe Tip:
If you're not handy at making meatballs of the same size, you can use a tablespoon to measure.

DIRECTIONS

1. Add half of the chopped onion into a large mixing bowl along with bread crumbs, cheese, oregano, pepper and 1 teaspoon of the salt. Mix with a fork until well combined.
2. Add the milk and mix well. Add the ground meat and egg. Knead the mixture by hand until all of the ingredients are evenly distributed - set aside.
3. Add the olive oil and the rest of the onions, carrot, and celery to the cooker and sauté. Pour in the tomato puree, salt, and water and mix well.
4. Move the bowl with the meat mixture next to the cooker and start making meatballs. As you shape each meatball, drop them into the cooker in an even layer.
5. Close the lid and set the valve to the pressure position.

   Stovetop & Electric Pressure Cook Time:
   5 minutes HIGH

6. When time is up, open the pressure cooker using the natural release method. Electric pressure cookers: Turn off the Keep Warm function and wait until the pressure indicator has gone down (about 20 to 30 minutes). Stovetop pressure cookers: Move the cooker off the burner and wait for the pressure to come down on its own (about 10 minutes).
7. Gently scoop meatballs out onto freshly cooked spaghetti and smother in tomato sauce.

Spicy Cherry Tomato Chicken Cacciatore

Make this recipe with bone-in chicken drumsticks, too. If you want to use chicken breasts, you should use bone-in, skin-on breasts only and follow the recommended cooking time.

Stovetop Pressure Cook Time
12 minutes HIGH

Electric Pressure Cook Time
15 minutes HIGH

Serves
4 - 6

INGREDIENTS

1 teaspoon olive oil
3 pounds bone-in chicken legs and thighs
1 pound cherry tomatoes
2 garlic cloves, crushed.
1 teaspoon hot pepper flakes (or one fresh hot pepper, chopped)
1 teaspoon salt (use 2 teaspoons if your chicken has not been previously salt-brined)
1 teaspoon dried oregano
¼ cup tart red table wine (such as Merlot)
1 cup water
½ cup pitted green olives, rinsed

Recipe Tip:
If using frozen skinless, boneless chicken breasts use only 1½ pounds and pressure cook for only 5 minutes.

DIRECTIONS

1. Add the olive oil to the cooker and brown the chicken thighs on all sides.
2. In the meantime, remove the stems from the cherry tomatoes and put them in a large Ziploc bag, so they are in a single layer. Close the bag almost completely - leave a tiny hole at the end. Or loosely knot a standard plastic bag. With a meat pounder, or heavy pot, lightly crush all the cherry tomatoes.
3. Set the chicken aside and pour the crushed cherry tomato mixture and all its juice into the cooker base. Add the garlic, hot pepper, salt, oregano, wine, and water and mix well, scraping up the brown bits of chicken stuck to the bottom of the cooker.
4. Place the chicken back into the cooker and mix to coat the chicken with the contents of the cooker. "Smooth" out the chicken pieces into an even layer. Close the lid and set the valve to the pressure position.

   Stovetop Pressure Cook Time:
   12 minutes HIGH

   Electric Pressure Cook Time:
   15 minutes HIGH

5. When time is up, release the pressure and open the lid. Stir the contents and let the cooker stand uncovered for about 5 minutes, occasionally stirring to reduce some of the cooking liquid.
6. Using a slotted spoon, lift into a serving casserole and sprinkle with green olives before serving. If desired, reserve the broth left in the base of the pressure cooker to use in place of stock in a future recipe.

Soy-Braised Beef Ribs

MEAT

Stovetop Pressure Cook Time
45 minutes HIGH

Electric Pressure Cook Time
60 minutes HIGH

Serves
4 - 6

Make this same recipe with pork ribs by cutting down the pressure cooking time to 25 minutes for electric and 20 minutes for stovetop pressure cookers!

INGREDIENTS

1 tablespoon sesame oil
2 cloves garlic, peeled and smashed
1" fresh ginger, peeled and finely chopped
1 pinch red pepper flakes
¼ cup rice vinegar (or white balsamic vinegar)
⅓ cup raw sugar
⅔ cup soy sauce
⅔ cup salt-free beef stock
4 pounds beef ribs (about 8), the butcher to saw or chop them in half
2 tablespoons cornstarch
1-2 tablespoons water

DIRECTIONS

1. Add the sesame oil garlic, ginger and red pepper flakes to the cooker and sauté for a minute.
2. De-glaze with vinegar, mix in the sugar, soy sauce, and beef stock - mix well. Add the ribs to the pressure cooker coating them with the mixture.
3. Close the lid and set the valve to the pressure position.

Stovetop Pressure Cook Time:
45 minutes HIGH

Electric Pressure Cook Time:
60 minutes HIGH

4. When time is up, open the pressure cooker using the natural release method. Electric pressure cookers: Turn off the Keep Warm function and wait until the pressure indicator has gone down (about 20 to 30 minutes). Stovetop pressure cookers: Move the cooker off the burner and wait for the pressure to come down on its own (about 10 minutes).
5. Remove the ribs from the cooker, leaving the cooking liquid inside, and place on an oven pan (they will not look very dark yet, this is ok). Slide under the broiler for about 5 minutes to brown (which will change their color to a rich dark brown).
6. In the meantime, make a slurry in a small container with the corn starch and water and then mix into the rib cooking liquid in the cooker.
7. Boil the mixture in the cooker until it reaches the desired consistency and then pour over the ribs before serving with steamed white rice.

Ground Beef Cottage Pie

Stovetop Pressure Cook Time
10 minutes HIGH

Electric Pressure Cook Time
12 minutes HIGH

Serves
4 - 6

Substitute the beef for lamb, and you've got Shepard's Pie! No need to change any other ingredients or cooking times.

Note: You will need to use your oven to complete this recipe.

INGREDIENTS

Meat Filling:

3 tablespoons unsalted butter, divided
1 large yellow onion, roughly diced medium
1½ pounds ground beef or lamb
2 large carrots, roughly diced
1 tablespoon tomato paste
1 tablespoon Worcestershire sauce (optional)
1 teaspoon salt (if using salt-free stock)
¼ teaspoon ground pepper
1 sprig fresh thyme leaves
1 cup stock, any kind
½ teaspoon apple cider vinegar
1 cup frozen peas

Mashed Potato Topping:

1½ pounds (about 4 medium) potatoes, sliced into 2" pieces
½ cup milk
½ teaspoon salt

Recipe Tip:
Substitute the beef for lamb and you've got Shepard's Pie! No need to change any other ingredients or cooking times.

DIRECTIONS

1. Melt 1 tablespoon of butter in the cooker over medium heat and add onion, sauté until onion is soft. Push the onion aside and drop in the ground meat- break it up with a spatula and brown it.
2. Add the carrots, tomato paste, Worcestershire Sauce (if using), salt, pepper, thyme sprig, and stock. Mix well.
3. Add the sliced potatoes to the steamer basket, lower the trivet and steamer basket onto the meat. Close the lid and set the valve to the pressure position.

Stovetop Pressure Cook Time:	Electric Pressure Cook Time:
10 minutes HIGH	12 minutes HIGH

4. When time is up, release the pressure and open the cooker.
5. Preheat oven to 400°F (200°C). Remove the steamer basket from the pressure cooker and toss a cup of frozen peas into the cooker and mix into the meat.
6. Remove the thyme sprig and let the cooker stand un-covered while you tumble the potatoes into a small mixing bowl.
7. Pull on the corners of the potato skins (with fingers or tongs) and peel off the potato skin and discard (or keep if you prefer). Splash the potatoes with milk and sprinkle with salt. Then mash until fluffy.
8. Pour the contents of the cooker into a prepared deep oven-safe dish (about 10" x 13"). Using a fork, add potatoes over the meat mixture starting at the edge of the dish and working your way into the center. Then squash with the back of the fork into an even layer.
9. Sprinkle the top with 2 tablespoons of chopped butter and slide into the oven. Bake, UN-covered for 20 minutes - or until the peaks of the potatoes have browned.
10. Remove from oven and let the casserole stand for 5 minutes before serving.

Chicken & Rice

A classic combination that is sure to please. Keep in mind, this recipe will require releasing pressure and then bringing the cooker back to pressure for additional time.

Stovetop Pressure Cook Time
12 minutes HIGH
+ 3 minutes HIGH

Electric Pressure Cook Time
14 minutes HIGH
+ 3 minutes HIGH

Makes
4 - 6

Accessories
4-cup capacity liquid measuring cup

INGREDIENTS

For the Chicken:

1 tablespoon olive oil
1 onion, chopped
1 clove garlic, minced
1 teaspoon ginger powder
1 teaspoon cardamom powder
½ teaspoon ground black pepper
2 teaspoons cumin powder
2 teaspoons coriander powder
¼ teaspoon turmeric powder
1 cup water
3 teaspoons tomato paste
8 bone-in, skin-on chicken pieces (4 drumsticks & 4 thighs)
2 bay leaves
3 teaspoons salt (decrease if using salt-brined chicken)

For the rice:

About 1 cup water (see instructions)
2 cups Basmati rice, rinsed
¼ cup raisins
¼ cup pine nuts
1-2 fresh tomatoes, chopped
1 wedge white onion, thinly sliced

Recipe Tip:
If you want a little more flavor and some added crunch to your chicken, leave the skin on.

DIRECTIONS

1. In the cooker, add oil and onion, sauté until soft. Add the garlic, ginger, cardamom, black pepper, cumin, coriander, and turmeric; stir everything around for about 30 seconds.
2. Add the water, tomato paste, and salt. Finally, add chicken pieces and coat in cooking liquid. Close the lid and set the valve to the pressure position.

Stovetop Pressure Cook Time:
12 minutes HIGH

Electric Pressure Cook Time:
14 minutes HIGH

3. When time is up, release the pressure and open the lid. Strain out the chicken pieces and place in a heatproof serving platter, and cover with foil.
4. Pour the cooking liquid from the cooker into a heat-proof 4-cup measuring cup to reach 3½ cups. If the cooking liquid does not reach 3½ cup mark add water. If you have more cooking liquid than 3½ cups reserve it for later use.
5. Pour the measured liquid back into the pressure cooker and add the rice. Close the lid and set the valve to the pressure position.

Stovetop & Electric Pressure Cook Time:
3 minutes HIGH

6. When time is up, open the pressure cooker using the natural release method. Electric pressure cookers: Turn off the Keep Warm function and wait until the pressure indicator has gone down (about 20 to 30 minutes). Stovetop pressure cookers: Move the cooker off the burner and wait for the pressure to come down on its own (about 10 minutes).
7. While the rice is cooking, slide the un-covered serving platter with chicken pieces skin-side up under broiler until the skin is brown and bubbly.
8. Temporarily transfer chicken and cooking liquid, if any, into the foil that was used to cover it and tumble the freshly pressure cooked rice onto the platter. Now add the chicken pieces on top and sprinkle with pine nuts, raisins, fresh tomato and onions before serving.

Michoacán-style Carnitas – Pulled Pork

Use this shredded pork to fill tamales, burritos, tacos, and quesadillas! If using stewing pork already cut into 1" cubes, halve the pressure cooking time – although this will cook faster the "shreds" will be shorter.

Stovetop Pressure Cook Time
30 minutes HIGH

Electric Pressure Cook Time
40 minutes HIGH

Serves
6 - 8

INGREDIENTS

2 tablespoons vegetable oil
1 large onion, roughly chopped
4 pounds pork roast, leg or shoulder sliced into 2" pieces
2 teaspoons cumin
1 teaspoon red pepper flakes
1 bay leaf
1 teaspoon salt
1 cup water

MEAT

DIRECTIONS

1. Add the oil and onion to the cooker and sauté. When the onions have almost softened, mix in the cumin, pepper flakes, and bay leaf.
2. Add the pork, water, and salt. Close the lid and set the valve to the pressure position.

   Stovetop Pressure Cook Time:
   30 minutes HIGH

   Electric Pressure Cook Time:
   40 minutes HIGH

3. When time is up, open the pressure cooker using the natural release method. Electric pressure cookers: Turn off the Keep Warm function and wait until the pressure indicator has gone down (about 20 to 30 minutes). Stovetop pressure cookers: Move the cooker off the burner and wait for the pressure to come down on its own (about 10 minutes).
4. Pull out the meat and place on a parchment-covered oven pan. Pull the cooked meat strips using two forks and arrange in a flat layer.
5. Slide the oven pan under the broiler for about 5 minutes to lightly singe the meat before serving.

Recipe Tip:
It isn't necessary to brown the meat at the beginning of the recipe because you're going to broil it at the end.

Skinny Turkey Sloppy Joes

Make this with your favorite ground meat without changing the cooking time.

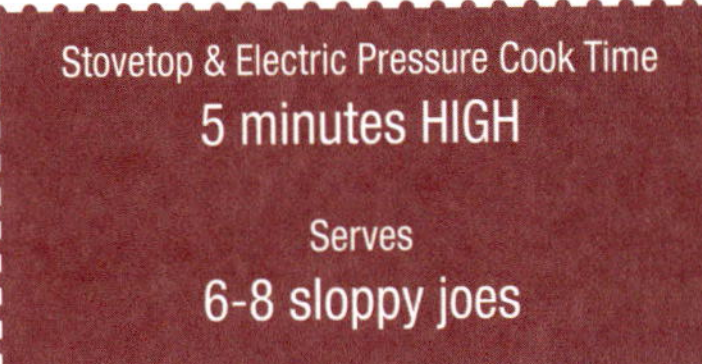

INGREDIENTS

1 tablespoon olive oil
1 pound ground turkey
1 medium red onion, chopped
1 medium green or red bell pepper, chopped
1 carrot, grated
1½ teaspoons salt
2 teaspoons garlic powder
1 tablespoon Worcestershire Sauce - optional
4 tablespoons apple cider vinegar
1 cup chopped tomatoes - canned or fresh with their juice
4 tablespoons tomato paste
1 cup water
½ cup rolled oats (or ¼ cup quick-cooking steel-cut oats)

DIRECTIONS

1. Add the ground turkey to the cooker and brown well. Push the meat aside and add onions, peppers, carrots, salt, and garlic powder and sauté until the veggies are soft (about 5 minutes).
2. Add the Worcestershire sauce, vinegar, chopped tomatoes, tomato paste, and water and mix well - lifting-up any brown bits of meat from the base of the cooker into the mixture.
3. When the contents of the cooker come to a boil, sprinkle the oats on top and do not stir. Close the lid and set the valve to the pressure position.

   Stovetop & Electric Pressure Cook Time:
   5 minutes HIGH

4. When time is up, release the pressure and open the cooker. Reduce the contents, continually stirring, for 5 minutes. Let mixture stand for an additional 5 minutes to thicken before serving.

Buffalo Chicken Wings

Inspired by the classic Buffalo Chicken Wings, instead of fried these wings are steamed in the pressure cooker, and then broiled. They won't be crispy, but singeing them under the broiler will give them a lightly dry and crunchy exterior. If doubling this recipe, do not jam more wings in the steamer basket - as they will not cook evenly - use a second steamer basket and place it on top of the first one.

Stovetop Pressure Cook Time
8 minutes HIGH

Electric Pressure Cook Time
10 minutes HIGH

Serves
4 - 6

Accessories
Steamer basket & trivet

MEAT

INGREDIENTS

2 pounds chicken wings (about 12), cut at the joint to make about 24 pieces
1 tablespoon olive oil
3 teaspoons salt, divided
4 tablespoons hot sauce
¼ cup honey
¼ cup tomato puree

DIRECTIONS

1. Coat the chicken wings with olive oil and one teaspoon of salt.
2. Add 1 cup of water to the cooker, place the trivet and a steamer basket in the cooker.
3. If the chicken wings are still whole, separate each into two by slicing through the skin to the joint, then bending the wing joint backward and slicing apart.
4. Place the chicken wings evenly spaced on the steamer basket - standing them up on their ends vertically if needed. Close the lid and set the valve to the pressure position.

   Stovetop Pressure Cook Time:
   8 minutes HIGH

   Electric Pressure Cook Time:
   10 minutes HIGH

5. While the chicken is cooking, prepare a large bowl with hot sauce, honey, tomato puree, and remaining salt. Mix the contents of the bowl well with a fork until the honey has completely dissolved.
6. When time is up, release the pressure and open the lid. Remove the chicken and tumble into the bowl, cover well.
7. Place wings on parchment-covered paper and cover with any remaining sauce. Slide under the broiler for about 5 minutes - or until brown and crispy.

Moroccan Lamb

Turn this into a one-pot meal, by using the cooking liquid to make couscous.

Stovetop Pressure Cook Time
25 minutes HIGH

Electric Pressure Cook Time
30 minutes HIGH

Serves
4

INGREDIENTS

10 ounces pitted prunes, soaked in hot water
1 tablespoon sesame seed oil
2 medium onions, roughly chopped
1 teaspoon cinnamon powder
1 teaspoon ginger powder
1 teaspoon turmeric powder
2½ pounds lamb shoulder, cut into pieces
1 cup vegetable stock
1 teaspoon salt, (if using unsalted stock)
3 tablespoons honey
1 bay laurel leaf
1 teaspoon pepper
1½ teaspoons salt
3½ ounces almonds, shelled, peeled and toasted
1 tablespoon sesame seeds

DIRECTIONS

1. Put the dried prunes in a bowl, and cover with boiling water cover, set aside.
2. Add sesame seed oil and onions to the cooker; let them cook until softened (about 3 minutes). Sprinkle in the cinnamon, turmeric, cumin, and ginger.
3. Push the onions to one side, add the meat and lightly brown. Pour in the vegetable stock, honey, salt (if using) and bay leaf. Scrape the bottom of the cooker well and maneuver the onions to somewhat cover the lamb.
4. Close the lid and set the valve to the pressure position.

   Stovetop Pressure Cook Time:
   25 minutes HIGH

   Electric Pressure Cook Time:
   30 minutes HIGH

5. When time is up, open the pressure cooker using the natural release method. Electric pressure cookers: Turn off the Keep Warm function and wait until the pressure indicator has gone down (about 20 to 30 minutes). Stovetop pressure cookers: Move the cooker off the burner and wait for the pressure to come down on its own (about 10 minutes).
6. Fish out the bay leaf and move to a serving platter. Sprinkle with toasted almonds and sesame seeds and serve.

Chapter Seven

VEGGIES

Veggies flash-cook in the pressure cooker. It's essential to open the pressure cooker as soon as they're done (unless otherwise noted in the recipe). If the vegetables are too tender for your liking, follow the same recommended cooking time but use the "Low" pressure setting instead.

Corn on the Cob

The pressure cooker steams the corn, cooking every kernel perfectly and leaving them filled with corn juice!

Stovetop & Electric Pressure Cook Time
2 minutes HIGH

Serves
4 - 8

INGREDIENTS

8 ears corn
1 cup water

DIRECTIONS

1. Husk the corns, cut off the bottom "stub" and wash thoroughly. Add the water to the cooker and arrange the corn vertically, with the larger end in the water and the smaller end up. Do not crowd the corn cobs - leave space around ears for steam to get there and cook the kernels evenly.
   Close the lid and set the valve to the pressure position.

   Stovetop & Electric Pressure Cook Time:
   2 minutes HIGH
2. When time is up, release the pressure and open the cooker. Serve with lots of butter and salt.

Recipe Tip:
If the ear is too tall for the cooker, lay it diagonally or snap it in half and put the wider end onto the base of the pressure cooker.

Spaghetti Squash and Easy Tomato Sauce One Pot

In this recipe, we make the sauce, and tenderize a Spaghetti Squash at the same time, making this a true one-pot meal!

Stovetop & Electric Pressure Cook Time
4 minutes HIGH

Makes
4

INGREDIENTS

1 tablespoon olive oil
1 medium onion, roughly sliced
1 (14 ounce) can chopped tomatoes (or 1 ¾ cups fresh chopped tomatoes)
1 teaspoon garlic powder
½ teaspoon red pepper flakes
½ cup water
1 teaspoon salt
1 medium spaghetti squash (about 4 pounds), halved and de-seeded

DIRECTIONS

1. Add the oil and onion to the cooker to brown. Add the chopped tomatoes, garlic powder, hot pepper flakes, water, and salt.
2. Position the spaghetti squash halves cut-side up into the tomato sauce.

   Stovetop & Electric Pressure Cook Time:
   4 minutes HIGH

3. When time is up, release the pressure and open the lid. Carefully lift out the squash and shred the pulp into individual dishes – while the sauce is reducing on low heat.
4. Top each squash with a portion of tomato sauce and a generous sprinkle of Parmigiano Reggiano cheese. Serve.

Recipe Tip:
To cook just the squash, simply replace the ingredients with 1 cup of water to steam the squash. The pressure cooking time remains the same.

Broccoli & Skin-on Potato Mash

No need to worry about cooking the potatoes and broccoli separately for this recipe, throw them all in together for a delicious side dish in minutes.

Stovetop & Electric Pressure Cook Time
5 minutes HIGH

Makes
4 - 6

INGREDIENTS

1½ cups water
2 pounds potatoes, sliced into 1" pieces
8 ounces broccoli florets
½ teaspoon salt
1 garlic clove, minced
½ cup cheddar cheese, shredded

DIRECTIONS

1. Add the water and potatoes in an even layer to the cooker. On top, sprinkle the broccoli florets. Close the lid and set the valve to the pressure position.

   Stovetop & Electric Pressure Cook Time:
   5 minutes HIGH

2. When time is up, release the pressure and open the lid. Sprinkle in the salt and the raw garlic. Mash and serve with a sprinkling of cheddar cheese.

Recipe Tip:
You can make this recipe with your favorite kind of white or golden potatoes without adjusting amount or cooking time.

Half-baked Potatoes

Make baked potatoes, but in half the time by steaming them in the pressure cooker while the oven is pre-heating!

INGREDIENTS

½ cup water
2 pounds (about 6) medium baking potatoes (Idaho or "old potatoes"), well-scrubbed

DIRECTIONS

1. Pierce the washed potatoes with a fork a few times and place them in the cooker.
2. Turn on oven to 450°F/245°C to pre-heat while the potatoes are pressure cooking.
3. Add the water over the potatoes. Close the lid and set the valve to the pressure position.

   Stovetop Pressure Cook Time: 8 minutes HIGH

   Electric Pressure Cook Time: 10 minutes HIGH

4. When time is up, release the pressure and open the lid. Using tongs, and being careful not to remove too much of the skin, remove the potatoes from the cooker.
5. Place each potato directly on the middle rack of the oven (poked holes facing up) and bake for 10-15 minutes - take out the smallest potatoes and serve first.
6. Turn off the oven and let the larger potatoes continue to bake using the oven's residual heat for another 5-10 minutes. Enjoy your crispy, fluffy baked short-cut potatoes!

Recipe Tip:
Since some ovens heat up much quicker than others, you will be the best judge of how much time your oven needs to properly pre-heat. Work accordingly.

Tomato Soup

A classic for a cold day, we recommend serving this with a grilled cheese sandwich!

Stovetop & Electric Pressure Cook Time
5 minutes HIGH

Makes
4 - 6

INGREDIENTS

4 tablespoons butter
2 pinches black pepper
1 medium carrot, roughly chopped
1 medium onion, roughly sliced
1 medium potato, roughly diced
1 (28 ounce) can high-quality whole canned tomatoes in their juice
3 tablespoons tomato paste or concentrate (2x or 3x strength)
3 tablespoons sun-dried tomatoes (if in oil, rinsed), roughly chopped
4 cups water
2 teaspoons salt

For garnish:
Fresh or sour cream or plain yogurt (to taste)

DIRECTIONS

1. Add the butter, pepper, onions, and carrots to the cooker and sauté. Stir occasionally until the onions start to soften (about 5 minutes).
2. Add the potatoes, canned tomatoes, tomato paste, sun-dried tomatoes, water, and salt. Close the lid and set the valve to the pressure position.

   Stovetop & Electric Pressure Cook Time:
   5 minutes HIGH

3. When time is up, open the pressure cooker using the natural release method. Electric pressure cookers: Turn off the Keep Warm function and wait until the pressure indicator has gone down (about 20 to 30 minutes). Stovetop pressure cookers: Move the cooker off the burner and wait for the pressure to come down on its own (about 10 minutes).
4. Using an immersion blender, blend the contents of the cooker until smooth. Serve with a twirl of fresh or sour cream.

Pumpkin Soup

A simple recipe, made even simpler if you use the fresh pre-cut pumpkin you can now find at the supermarket!

Stovetop & Electric Pressure Cook Time
10 minutes HIGH

Makes
4 - 6

INGREDIENTS

1 tablespoon olive oil
1 large onion, roughly chopped
1 sprig of sage
½" piece of fresh ginger, peeled and roughly sliced
4 pounds pumpkin, peeled, seeded and cubed
¼ teaspoon, nutmeg
4 cups vegetable stock
olive oil
½ cup of toasted pumpkin seeds, for garnish

DIRECTIONS

1. Add the oil, onions, sage, and ginger to the cooker and sauté. When the onions are soft, scoot onions aside and tumble in enough pumpkin cubes to cover the base of the cooker (about a handful), let brown for about 10 minutes stirring infrequently.
2. Tumble in the rest of the gourd along with the ginger, nutmeg, and stock. Close the lid and set the valve to the pressure position.

   Stovetop & Electric Pressure Cook Time:
   10 minutes HIGH

3. When time is up, release the pressure and open the cooker. Fish out the woody sage stem and discard.
4. With a stick immersion blender, puree the contents of the pressure cooker and serve. Garnish with salted, toasted pumpkin seeds.

Chapter Eight

CONDIMENTS, JAMS & DRINKS

Homemade Soy Milk

The vanilla bean will very lightly infuse the milk and make it taste not so "beany" - it will not taste like vanilla milk. For a more definitive vanilla flavor, add a drop of vanilla extract before bottling.

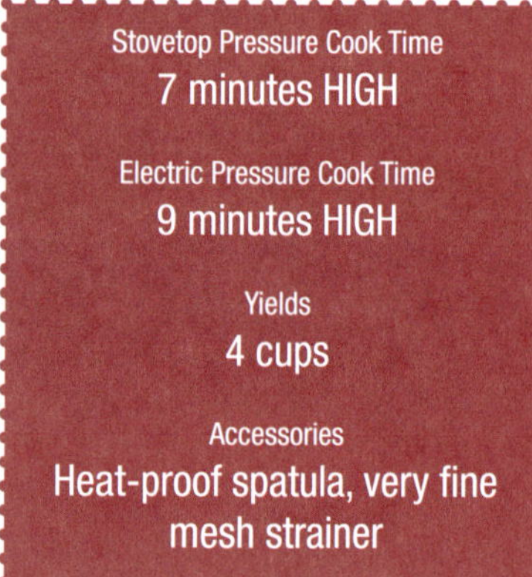

INGREDIENTS

½ cup organic yellow soybeans
5 cups water, plus more for blending
½ teaspoon raw sugar (optional)
1 vanilla bean (optional)
1 pinch sea salt (optional)

DIRECTIONS

1. Soak the yellow soybeans 24 to 36 hours in abundant water. Strain, rinse, and change the water about half-way through this soaking period (or every 12 hours if soaking longer). Strain and rinse the soy beans before using.
2. In a small food chopper or processor add the soaked soybeans and ½ a cup of water. Puree the beans and water at the highest setting (liquefy and/or turbo) for 90 seconds. Plop the raw soy pulp into the cooker.
3. Add the 5 cups of water and mix everything together well - ensure that the contents of the cooker do not exceed more than half the pot capacity.

Recipe Tip:
Save the soy bean pulp (or Okara) from this recipe for making other dishes such as homemade bread.

4. Bring the uncovered pressure cooker to a boil stirring occasionally. You will know the soy is boiling when the foam increases in volume quickly.
5. Remove the foam from the top and discard, then wipe down the sides of the pot with a spatula and give the contents one last stir. Close the lid and set the valve to the pressure position.

Stovetop Pressure Cook Time:
7 minutes HIGH

Electric Pressure Cook Time:
9 minutes HIGH

6. In the meantime, in a wide-mouth pitcher or bowl, add the sugar, vanilla bean, and salt (if using) and place a fine-mesh strainer on top.
7. When time is up, open the pressure cooker using the natural release method. Electric pressure cookers: Turn off the Keep Warm function and wait until the pressure indicator has gone down (about 20 to 30 minutes). Stovetop pressure cookers: Move the cooker off the burner and wait for the pressure to come down on its own (about 10 minutes).
8. Carefully pour the hot contents of the cooker through the fine-mesh strainer into the pitcher, pushing down on the pulp with the spatula to wring out any remaining milk from the pulp.
9. Mix the contents in the pitcher well and let cool and then remove and rinse off the vanilla bean to use for your next batch.
10. Cover tightly and refrigerate - keeps for 3-4 days in the refrigerator. Shake, or mix, before using.

Plum BBQ Sauce

This recipe can be doubled, and even tripled if the pressure cooker is not more than ½ full (because of the dried fruit).

Stovetop & Electric Pressure Cook Time
10 minutes HIGH

Makes
About 1 ½ cups BBQ sauce

Accessories
Immersion blender

INGREDIENTS

1 tablespoon sesame seed oil (or any other high smoke-pint oil such as peanut, avocado or grapeseed)
1 medium onion, roughly chopped
½ cup tomato puree
½ cup water
4 tablespoons honey
4 tablespoons white vinegar (or apple cider vinegar)
1 teaspoon sea salt
½ teaspoon garlic powder
1 teaspoon hot sauce,
1 teaspoon liquid smoke
⅛ teaspoon ground clove powder
⅛ teaspoon cumin powder
¾ cup seedless dried plums (aka prunes), tightly packed in a measuring cup

DIRECTIONS

1. Add the sesame oil and onion to the cooker and sauté occasionally stirring until the edges of the onion start to brown.
2. In a 2-cup measuring cup, or small mixing bowl, pour in the tomato puree, water, honey, and vinegar using the measuring lines on the cup as a guideline.
3. Add the salt, garlic, hot sauce, liquid smoke, clove, and cumin powders to the mixture. Mix the contents of the measuring cup well, so that the honey dissolves evenly in the liquid.
4. Pour the mixture into the cooker, rubbing the base of the cooker with the spatula to lift-up any browned onion bits into the sauce.
5. Tumble in the plums. Close the lid and set the valve to the pressure position.

Stovetop & Electric Pressure Cook Time:

10 minutes HIGH

6. When time is up, release the pressure and open the lid.
7. Using an immersion blender, and tilting the pot so the blender is immersed in the liquid, puree the contents of the cooker.

Spicy Mango Chutney

When pressure cooking fruit, remember not to fill the pressure cooker more than halfway with all ingredients and only open the cooker using the natural release method.

Stovetop Pressure Cook Time
7 minutes HIGH

Electric Pressure Cook Time
5 minutes HIGH

Makes
About 2 cups

INGREDIENTS

1 tablespoon vegetable oil
1 shallot, chopped
2 tablespoons fresh ginger, finely diced
¼ teaspoon cardamom powder
⅛ teaspoon cinnamon
2 fresh red hot chili, finely chopped
(or ½ teaspoon red pepper flakes)
2 large mangoes, diced
1 apple, cored and diced (skin-on)
¼ cup raisins
2 teaspoons salt
1¼ cups raw (demerara) sugar
1¼ cups apple cider vinegar
(or 1 cup white wine vinegar)

CONDIMENTS

Recipe Tip:
The pressure cooking time for electric cookers is shorter in this recipe because the natural pressure release method takes longer.

DIRECTIONS

1. Add the vegetable oil, shallots, and ginger to the cooker and sauté until the shallots begin to soften.
2. Add the cardamom, cinnamon, and hot peppers and sauté for about a minute to fry and bloom the spices. Add the remaining ingredients to the pressure cooker and mix well until all of the sugar has melted.
3. Close the lid and set the valve to the pressure position.

Stovetop Pressure Cook Time:	Electric Pressure Cook Time:
7 minutes HIGH	5 minutes HIGH

4. When time is up, open the pressure cooker using the natural release method. Electric pressure cookers: Turn off the Keep Warm function and wait until the pressure indicator has gone down (about 20 to 30 minutes). Stovetop pressure cookers: Move the cooker off the burner and wait for the pressure to come down on its own (about 10 minutes).
5. Simmer the un-covered pressure cooker on medium heat (sauté or brown functions for electric pressure cookers) until the contents have a jam-like consistency - you can drag the spoon across the base and see it (about 15 minutes).
6. Stir occasionally, at first, and then as the mixture gets thicker, you will want to turn down the heat and stir more frequently. For electric cookers, go from the Brown/Sauté function to the Keep Warm function.
7. Spoon piping hot chutney into clean jars and close tightly. When cooled refrigerate for up to a month or transfer to freezer-safe containers to freeze up to a year.

Hip Ketchup

With this recipe, you're guaranteed to never run out of ketchup during those summer BBQs or big family get-togethers.

Stovetop & Electric Pressure Cook Time
5 minutes HIGH

Makes
About 4 cups

Accessories
Potato masher & immersion blender

INGREDIENTS

2 pounds plum tomatoes, sliced into quarters
1 tablespoon paprika
1 teaspoon salt
1/8 teaspoon cinnamon
1/8 teaspoon clove powder
1/8 teaspoon garlic powder
1/4 teaspoon celery seeds
1/2 teaspoon Dijon mustard
1 tablespoon honey
1/3 cup raisins
1/8 onion, wedged
6 tablespoons apple cider vinegar
Optional: 1 tablespoon corn starch + 1 tablespoon of water

DIRECTIONS

1. Put all of the ingredients into the cooker except for the corn starch and water. Use a potato masher and squish everything (it won't truly mash because the tomatoes are not cooked) until enough liquid comes out of the tomatoes for the cooker to reach pressure (1/2 to 1 cup).
2. Close the lid and set the valve to the pressure position.

   Stovetop & Electric Pressure Cook Time:
   5 minutes HIGH

3. When time is up, release the pressure and open the lid. Let simmer uncovered for at least 10 minutes or until it is almost reduced by half (there is no need to stir).
4. If using, mix corn starch with water into a slurry and pour into the tomato mixture. Using an immersion blender, puree the contents until smooth.
5. Pour into a freshly-cleaned or sterilized glass bottle or jar and seal. Let cool and refrigerate before using - it keeps in the refrigerator for about 3 months. Or, once cooled, transfer into a Ziploc bag to freeze for up to one year.

Recipe Tip:
If you'd like commercial-quality smooth ketchup, simply pass through a sieve - but this is not necessary it's still plenty smooth when blended with an immersion blender.

1-Minute Hip Hot Sauce

Never too hot, homemade hot sauce heats things up the way you like it.

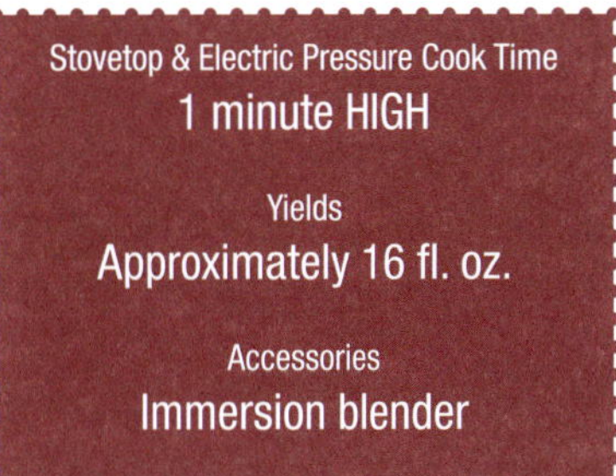

INGREDIENTS

12 ounces fresh hot peppers (any kind), stems removed
1¼ cup apple cider vinegar or as needed (or whatever kind you prefer)
2 teaspoons smoked salt (or plain)
2 teaspoons liquid smoke – if using plain salt

DIRECTIONS

1. Roughly chop the peppers and add to the cooker. Add enough vinegar to cover, and salt. Close the lid and set the valve to the pressure position.

   Stovetop & Electric Pressure Cook Time:
   1 minute HIGH

2. When time is up, open the pressure cooker using the natural release method. Electric pressure cookers: Turn off the Keep Warm function and wait until the pressure indicator has gone down (about 20 to 30 minutes). Stovetop pressure cookers: Move the cooker off the burner and wait for the pressure to come down on its own (about 10 minutes).
3. Puree the contents with an immersion blender and strain into a sterilized or freshly dish-washed bottle. Keep refrigerated for up to 3 months, or transfer to a suitable container and freeze up to a year.

Recipe Tip:
For a traditionally bright red hot sauce, use only red hot peppers.

Quick Ricotta Cheese

The only thing better than cheese is homemade cheese!

Makes
Approximately 1 cup of ricotta

INGREDIENTS

1 quart high-quality whole milk – do not substitute
2-3 tablespoons white or apple cider vinegar
2 pinches salt

DIRECTIONS FOR ELECTRIC PRESSURE COOKER

1. Add the milk to the cooker, close the lid, and set the valve on the lid to "steam." Simmer about 10 minutes.
2. Remove the lid, and set to Brown. Stir constantly until you begin to see the milk foaming – small bubbles forming on the surface. Remove the insert from the pressure cooker and set on a trivet.
3. Add one tablespoon of vinegar to the milk and swish around delicately with the spatula. If it does not begin to break-up immediately, add another tablespoon.
4. Let the milk stand for 1 minute. Pour the mixture through a fine-mesh strainer.
5. Sprinkle two pinches of salt into the strainer, over the mixture, and use the spatula to gather and press the solids into a small form.
6. Let the quick-ricotta cool in the strainer and then store in a sealed container in the refrigerator for up to 3 days.

DIRECTIONS FOR STOVETOP PRESSURE COOKER

1. Add the milk to the pressure cooker and turn up the heat. Stir constantly until you begin to see the milk foaming – small bubbles forming on the surface. Turn off the heat.
2. Add one tablespoon of vinegar, and swish the milk around delicately with the spatula. If it does not begin to break-up immediately, add another.
3. Let the milk stand for 1 minute. Pour the mixture through a fine-mesh strainer.
4. Sprinkle two pinches of salt into the strainer, over the mixture, and use the spatula to gather and press the solids into a small form.
5. Let the quick-ricotta cool in the strainer and then store in a sealed container in the refrigerator for up to 3 days.

Recipe Tip:
When making this ricotta in an electric cooker, you don't have to constantly stir – the unit will bring the milk close to the right temperature and all you have to do is show up just before the milk is ready to boil.

zavor

Chapter Nine

DESSERTS & FRUIT

Most desserts in the pressure cooker require a heat-proof dish to "steam bake" – you probably already have something sufficient to use in your kitchen. If the item is heat-safe, or safe to use in the oven, then it is safe to use in your pressure cooker!

Limoncello Ricotta Cheesecake

Did you know that you can make a cheesecake in the pressure cooker without using a cheesecake pan? Any flat-bottomed heat-proof dish will work if it's lined with wax paper.

Stovetop Pressure Cook Time
15 minutes HIGH

Electric Pressure Cook Time
20 minutes HIGH

Serves
6 - 8

Accessories
Trivet & 7" heat proof, flat bottomed dish

INGREDIENTS

4 ounces Biscotti
2 tablespoons unsalted butter, half melted, half softened
2 tablespoons lemon zest, grated
6 ounces ricotta, drained, room temperature
8 ounces cream cheese, room temperature
⅓ cup sugar
¼ cup Limoncello liqueur (or lemon juice)
1 tablespoon vanilla extract
2 large eggs, room temperature, beaten
1 hazelnut chocolate bar

Recipe Tip:
Once the cake has cooled you can top it with a flat plate and flip it out. It will be upside-down, so all you need to do is to cover the bottom with the serving dish and flip one last time.

DESSERT & FRUIT

DIRECTIONS

1. About an hour before you begin your recipe pull the eggs, ricotta, and cream cheese out of the refrigerator to get them to room temperature.
2. Add one cup of water to the cooker and add the trivet and set aside.
3. Grab a square of softened butter and rub it around the bottom and edges of the heatproof dish, set aside.
4. In a small pan, melt the butter. Meanwhile, pulverize the biscotti, pour in the melted butter and pulse the chopper/processor once to incorporate.
5. Press the crumbs with the back of your fingers or a spoon to the bottom of the heatproof dish into a layer no thicker than ¼ inch. If you have extra crust, press it going up the sides as well. Place the container in the refrigerator to solidify the crust while you move on to the next steps.
6. In a mixing bowl with a hand blender, or with a fork stirring vigorously, break-up and mix the ricotta. Then, add the cream cheese and sugar. A little at a time, add the limoncello, vanilla, and lemon zest.
7. When everything is mixed together, add the beaten eggs. The result will be the consistency of a very runny pancake batter.
8. Take the cookie-crumb crust container out of the refrigerator, and delicately pour the cheese mixture over the crust. Lower this into the pressure cooker un-covered. Close the lid and set the valve to the pressure position.

   Stovetop Pressure Cook Time:
   15 minutes HIGH

   Electric Pressure Cook Time:
   20 minutes HIGH

9. When time is up, open the pressure cooker using the natural release method. Electric pressure cookers: Turn off the Keep Warm function and wait until the pressure indicator has gone down (about 20 to 30 minutes). Stovetop pressure cookers: Move the cooker off the burner and wait for the pressure to come down on its own (about 10 minutes).
10. Delicately remove the container and place on a cooling rack. Let the cake rest uncovered for about an hour and then refrigerate for another hour.
11. Shave a chocolate bar with a vegetable peeler to make hazelnut chocolate "splinters." Sprinkle hazelnut splinters on top of the cheesecake before serving.

DESSERT & FRUIT

Upside-Down Pear, Walnut & Ricotta Cake

Whenever making an upside-down cake, get artistic with the initial fruit arrangement. This is the design everyone will see once you flip it over, so have fun!

Stovetop & Electric Pressure Cook Time
20 minutes HIGH

Serves
6 - 8

Accessories
Trivet, 4-cup capacity heat-proof bowl

INGREDIENTS

2 pears, 1 sliced 1 diced
1 tablespoon lemon juice
⅛ teaspoon olive oil
¼ cup raw sugar
1 egg
1 cup ricotta cheese
⅓ cup white sugar
3 tablespoons extra-virgin olive oil
1 teaspoon vanilla extract
(or the seeds of one vanilla bean)
1 cup all-purpose flour
⅛ teaspoon cinnamon
2 teaspoons baking powder
1 teaspoon baking soda
¼ cup walnuts, chopped
¼ cup raisins

Recipe Tip:
This recipe only calls for a "hint" of cinnamon, however, if you really enjoy the flavor it brings, you can double it.

DIRECTIONS

1. Add 1 cup of water to cooker, place trivet into the pot and set aside.
2. Slice one pear and dice the other and cover with lemon juice.
3. Prepare a shallow and wide 4-cup capacity heat-proof bowl by adding a disk of wax paper to the bottom and rubbing oil on it. Sprinkle the base of the bowl with raw sugar in an even layer and arrange the sliced pears artistically.
4. In a small mixing bowl, mix the egg, ricotta, sugar, olive oil, and vanilla using a fork. Then, sprinkle the flour, cinnamon, baking powder, and baking soda in the mixing bowl using a flour sifter or fine mesh strainer. Blend well with a fork and then stir in the pear slices, walnuts, and raisins.
5. Pour the batter into the prepared bowl and lower into the pressure cooker, uncovered. Close the lid and set the valve to the pressure position.

   Stovetop & Electric Pressure Cook Time:
   20 minutes HIGH

6. When time is up, open the pressure cooker using the natural release method. Electric pressure cookers: Turn off the Keep Warm function and wait until the pressure indicator has gone down (about 20 to 30 minutes). Stovetop pressure cookers: Move the cooker off the burner and wait for the pressure to come down on its own (about 10 minutes).
7. Test for doneness by inserting a toothpick in the middle - if it comes out dirty lower back into the pressure and cook for a few more minutes.
8. Turn the cake out onto a serving plate. Serve warm or chilled.

Beanie Brownie Cake

The perfect recipe for satisfying your sweet tooth while staying healthy.

Stovetop Pressure Cook Time
10 minutes HIGH
+ 20 minutes HIGH

Electric Pressure Cook Time
12 minutes HIGH
+ 20 minutes HIGH

Serves
6 - 8

Accessories
Trivet, 4-cup capacity heat-proof bowl

INGREDIENTS

1 cup dry Pinto beans, soaked overnight
4 cups water

For Cake:

½ cup un-sweetened cocoa powder
½ cup raw honey
⅛ teaspoon pure almond extract
3 tablespoons extra virgin olive oil
2 large eggs
2 pinches (⅛ tsp) sea salt
2 teaspoons baking powder
Optional: ¼ cup sliced or slivered almonds

Recipe Tip:
This cake has a chocolate – fudgy consistency so don't be afraid to serve it with ice cream or just a cold glass of milk.

DIRECTIONS

1. Add the soaked, rinsed, and strained beans and water to the cooker. Close the lid and set the valve to the pressure position.

   Stovetop Pressure Cook Time:
   10 minutes HIGH

   Electric Pressure Cook Time:
   12 minutes HIGH

2. When time is up, open the pressure cooker using the natural release method. Electric pressure cookers: Turn off the Keep Warm function and wait until the pressure indicator has gone down (about 20 to 30 minutes). Stovetop pressure cookers: Move the cooker off the burner and wait for the pressure to come down on its own (about 10 minutes).
3. Strain the beans and place into a food processor and blend to almost a puree. Then wait for the beans to cool for about 10 more minutes.
4. In the meantime, rinse out the cooker and add one cup of water and trivet, and set aside.
5. Lightly coat a 4-cup capacity heat-proof bowl with olive oil, and an optional sprinkle of cocoa powder (this can get messy), and set aside.
6. Add the cocoa powder, honey, almond extract, olive oil, eggs, and salt into the food processor. Puree the contents of the processor at high speed until well combined, then add the baking powder and process for about a minute more.
7. Using a spatula transfer the contents of the processor into the heat-proof bowl. Lower the un-covered heat-proof bowl onto the steamer basket. Close the lid and set the valve to pressure cooking position.

   Stovetop & Eloctric Pressure Cook Time:
   20 minutes HIGH

8. When time is up, release the pressure and open the lid. Remove the cake and let cool for about 5 minutes before unmolding the cake onto a serving dish.
9. Let the cake cool uncovered another 10 minutes. Sprinkle the cake with sliced almonds if desired. Serve warm or chilled.

Caramelized Apple Crumb Cake

DESSERT & FRUIT

Whenever making an upside down-cake, get artistic with the initial fruit arrangement. This is the design everyone will see once you flip it over, so have fun!

Stovetop & Electric Pressure Cook Time
20 minutes HIGH

Serves
4 - 6

Accessories
Trivet, 4-cup capacity heat-proof bowl

INGREDIENTS

6 small yellow or red apples, cored and sliced cross-wise
¾ cup butter, melted
1 square of butter, softened
2 tablespoons flour
¼ cup of demerara/raw sugar

Crumb Filling:

2 cups dry bread crumbs
¾ cup sugar
1 teaspoon cinnamon
1 teaspoon ginger powder
½ lemon, juice and rind

Recipe Tip:
A flat bottom container is preferable, but you can certainly make this dessert in a bowl with a rounded bottom - it will require a little more skill to artistically arrange the apples on the "top" exterior layer.

DIRECTIONS:

1. Prepare the ingredients for the crumb filling by combining the bread crumbs, sugar, cinnamon, ginger, lemon juice, zest, and melted butter. Mix well and set aside.
2. Take your un-peeled, well-washed apples, and remove their core. Slice them very thinly - if possible, use a mandolin for nice, even, thin slices.
3. Butter the interior of the container all the way up to the edge. Put the tablespoons of flour in the container and swoosh the flour around so that you have an even coat of flour stuck to the butter inside the container.
4. Begin layering the apple slices. The bottom layer will become the top when you flip the cake out of the container so arrange the apple slices carefully for this. Add a layer of bread crumb mixture. Alternate apple and bread crumb layers until your container is full or you run out of ingredients. The other layers of apples do not need to be so carefully laid - just ensure that you have apple slices all the way to the edge of the container and in a relatively even layer.
5. When you are finished filling your container, cover tightly with tin foil. If your container does not have a handle that will facilitate putting it in and out of the cooker, construct a sling using aluminum foil.
6. Add 1 cup of water and the trivet to the cooker. Lower the container in, close the lid and set the valve to the pressure position.

   Stovetop & Electric Pressure Cook Time:

   20 minutes HIGH

7. When time is up, open the pressure cooker using the natural release method. Electric pressure cookers: Turn off the Keep Warm function and wait until the pressure indicator has gone down (about 20 to 30 minutes). Stovetop pressure cookers: Move the cooker off the burner and wait for the pressure to come down on its own (about 10 minutes).
8. Carefully lift the container from the cooker and remove the tin foil. Place your serving dish on top of the container and flip it upside-down so that the serving dish is now on the bottom.
9. Remove the heat-proof dish to reveal your beautiful apple cake!

Crustless Mini Pumpkin Pies

DESSERT & FRUIT

This recipe makes enough to fill eight 4oz ramekins.

Stovetop & Electric Pressure Cook Time
5 minutes HIGH
+ 8 minutes HIGH

Serves
6 - 8

Accessories
Steamer basket & trivet, ramekins

INGREDIENTS

2 pounds butternut squash, peeled and cubed
1 cup whole milk (or fresh cream, or coconut milk)
¾ cup 100% pure maple syrup
2 large eggs
1 teaspoon powdered cinnamon
½ teaspoon powdered ginger
(or 1" piece fresh ginger, peeled & very finely chopped)
¼ teaspoon powdered cloves
1 tablespoon organic corn starch
2 pinches sea salt

Garnish: sweetened whipped cream and chopped pecans

Recipe Tip:
You can freeze or refrigerate the remaining pumpkin pulp for future pumpkin pies or add it into a pasta sauce or soup.

DESSERT & FRUIT

DIRECTIONS

1. Add 1 cup water and the trivet to the cooker. Add the squash cubes to the steamer basket and lower into the cooker. Close the lid and set the valve to the pressure position.

   Stovetop & Electric Pressure Cook Time:
   5 minutes HIGH

2. In the meantime, in a 4-cup measuring cup, or medium mixing bowl, measure out the milk, maple syrup, and then add the eggs, cinnamon, ginger, salt, and corn starch. Beat using a fork or an immersion blender, until the ingredients are well combined.
3. When the pressure cooking time is up, release the pressure and open the lid. Tumble the cooked butternut squash in a fine-mesh strainer and, once cooled (about 10 minutes), press on the squash pulp to release some liquid (save this liquid to use in place of stock in other recipes).
4. Measure the strained pulp by pouring it into a 2-cup measuring cup. Scrape the pulp into the measuring cup with the egg mixture and blend well.
5. Add 1 cup water to the cooker along with the steamer basket and trivet and set aside. Pour the mixture into heat-proof ramekins and lower into the pressure cooker uncovered - put the second layer on top of the first by balancing on the edges of the ramekins below. Close the lid and set the valve to the pressure position.

   Stovetop & Electric Pressure Cook Time:
   8 minutes HIGH

6. When time is up, open the pressure cooker using the natural release method. Electric pressure cookers: Turn off the Keep Warm function and wait until the pressure indicator has gone down (about 20 to 30 minutes). Stovetop pressure cookers: Move the cooker off the burner and wait for the pressure to come down on its own (about 10 minutes).
7. Lift the ramekins out of the cooker using tongs and let stand 5 minutes before serving or allow it to cool entirely by covering tightly and refrigerating for up to two days.

Alice's Baked Apples

DESSERT & FRUIT

Baked apples are the perfect alternative to apple pie. You can use any kind of fresh apple for this recipe.

INGREDIENTS

6 fresh apples, cored
¼ cup raisins
1 cup red wine
¼ cup raw demerara sugar
1 teaspoon cinnamon powder

Stovetop & Electric Pressure Cook Time
10 minutes HIGH

Serves
6

Recipe Tip:
Apples that have been conserved in a controlled environment can look fresh but may be up to a year or more old. These "conserved" fresh apples will disintegrate completely for this recipe so be sure to use fresh ones.

DIRECTIONS

1. Add the apples to the base of the cooker. Pour in the wine, sprinkle raisins, sugar, and cinnamon powder. Close the lid and set the valve to the pressure position.

   Stovetop & Electric Pressure Cook Time:

   10 minutes HIGH

2. When time is up, open the pressure cooker using the natural release method. Electric pressure cookers: Turn off the Keep Warm function and wait until the pressure indicator has gone down (about 20 to 30 minutes). Stovetop pressure cookers: Move the cooker off the burner and wait for the pressure to come down on its own (about 10 minutes).
3. Scoop the apples out of the cooker and serve in a small bowl with lots of cooking liquid.

Light Tapioca Pudding

We skip the eggs in this recipe to keep it light and easy.

Stovetop Pressure Cook Time
10 minutes HIGH

Electric Pressure Cook Time
8 minutes HIGH

Serves
6 - 8

Accessories
Trivet, 4-cup capacity heat-proof bowl

INGREDIENTS

1/3 cup seed tapioca pearls
1¼ cups whole milk (or your favorite milk alternative)
½ cup water
½ cup sugar
½ lemon, zested

DIRECTIONS

1. Add one cup of water to the cooker and the trivet, set aside.
2. Rinse tapioca pearls in a fine-mesh strainer and pour into a 4-cup capacity heat-proof bowl. Add milk, water, lemon zest, and sugar. Mix well until the sugar has dissolved and you no longer feel the grit of it at the base of the bowl.
3. If the container does not have handles to easily lower and lift it from the pressure cooker, construct a foil sling. Lower the uncovered heat-proof bowl into the pressure cooker. Close the lid and set the valve to the pressure position.

   Stovetop Pressure Cook Time: 10 minutes HIGH

   Electric Pressure Cook Time: 8 minutes HIGH

4. When time is up, open the pressure cooker using the natural release method. Electric pressure cookers: Turn off the Keep Warm function and wait until the pressure indicator has gone down (about 20 to 30 minutes). Stovetop pressure cookers: Move the cooker off the burner and wait for the pressure to come down on its own (about 10 minutes).
5. Once the pressure has released let the mixture stand in the closed cooker for an additional 5 minutes before opening the lid (the milk in the container will boil over if you open the lid too quickly after pressure is released).
6. Carefully lift out the heat-proof bowl and stir the contents vigorously with a fork before distributing into serving bowls, glasses, or forms.
7. Cover the containers tightly with cling-wrap and let cool before refrigerating for at least 3 hours, or overnight.

Recipe Tip:
You can replace the lemon in this recipe with orange or ½ vanilla bean if you prefer.

Candied Lemon Peels

Eat them straight instead of candy, or use as a garnish for dessert.

INGREDIENTS:

1 pound organic lemons - about 5 lemons
2¼ cups white granulated sugar, divided
5 cups water, divided

DIRECTIONS:

1. Wash the lemons well using a scrubby sponge to clean the surface. Slice the lemon in half lengthwise and juice - reserve the juice for another use. Slice each lemon half in quarters. Hold the quarters flat on the cutting board, peel or slice out the pulp.
2. Slice the de-pulped lemon quarters into thin strips - about as wide as the lemon peel is thick. Add the lemon peel strips and four cups of water to the cooker. Close the lid and set the valve to the pressure position.

   Stovetop & Electric Pressure Cook Time:
   3 minutes HIGH

4. When time is up, release the pressure in short bursts and open the lid. Strain the lemon peel strips and rinse them. Then, discard cooking water and rinse out the cooker.
5. Add 2 cups sugar, 1 cup water, lemon strips on medium heat uncovered stirring occasionally until all of the sugar has melted - about 5 minutes. Close the lid and set the valve to the pressure position.

   Stovetop & Electric Pressure Cook Time:
   10 minutes HIGH

6. When time is up, open the pressure cooker using the natural release method. Electric pressure cookers: Turn off the Keep Warm function and wait until the pressure indicator has gone down (about 20 to 30 minutes). Stovetop pressure cookers: Move the cooker off the burner and wait for the pressure to come down on its own (about 10 minutes).
7. Strain peels, saving the delicate syrup, if you'd like, for another use, and spread the peels on a cutting board or parchment paper to cool for 15 minutes or more.
8. Gently toss four to five peels at a time in a small plate of sugar to coat. Shake off the excess and lay them down on a new parchment on a sheet-pan that can fit in your refrigerator.
9. Put the sheet pan with the sugared-coated candied lemon peels in the refrigerator uncovered for at least 4 hours to dry completely -overnight is even better. Move the strips to a glass jar for storage in a cool dry place for 6-8 weeks - or keep refrigerated for up to six months.

zavor.
MEAT
SLOW COOK
MENU
START/STOP
KEEP WARM

Chapter Ten

SLOW COOK

Low-temperature recipes that will make your mouth water. Exclusive for users with electric multi-cookers.

Broccoli Cheddar Soup

Slow Cooking Time
1.5 hours HIGH

Serves
4 - 6

INGREDIENTS

1 tablespoon butter
½ cup shredded carrots
1 medium onion, diced
2 heads of broccoli cut into small florets
4 cups chicken broth
1 cup water
1½ tablespoon minced garlic
4 cups reduced fat sharp cheddar cheese, shredded
1 can evaporated milk
¼ cup all-purpose flour

DIRECTIONS

1. Heat the butter in the cooker; add the onions and garlic and sauté. Add in the water, chicken broth, carrots, broccoli, and flour.
2. Close the lid and set the valve to the STEAM position.
3. Slow Cook on HIGH for 1½ hours.
4. Once the time is up, open the lid and stir in the evaporated milk. Then slowly add in the cheddar cheese a little bit at a time until it is thoroughly mixed in.
5. Serve in bread bowls.

Sweet Corn Chowder

The perfect recipe for summer and winter. For a creamier version, stir in 1 cup sour cream before serving.

Slow Cooking Time
6 hours LOW

Serves
6

INGREDIENTS

3 cups fresh corn kernels
1 tablespoon butter
1 clove garlic, minced
½ cup diced red bell pepper
2 cups peeled and diced white potatoes
¾ cup diced celery
⅓ cup diced onion
2 cups chicken stock
½ teaspoon dried thyme
¼ teaspoon cayenne pepper (or to taste)

DIRECTIONS

1. Heat the butter in the cooker and brown the corn for 10 minutes.
2. Add the remaining ingredients and stir well.
3. Close the lid and set the valve to the STEAM position.
4. Slow cook on LOW 6 hours.
5. Serve with crusty French bread.

SLOW COOK

Recipe Tip:
This recipe calls for fresh corn, frozen corn will still work but the results won't be as sweet.

Easy Sweet and Sour Chicken

This popular recipe works better in a slow cooker than a pressure cooker – because it can remain unattended for longer. That extra time means the flavors will be more concentrated, and a simple dinner is waiting for you when you get home.

Slow Cooking Time
6 hours LOW

Serves
4

SLOW COOK

Recipe Tip:
For a healthier alternative, serve this recipe with steamed broccoli rather than rice.

INGREDIENTS

1½ pounds diced boneless skinless chicken
1½ cups diced bell pepper
1 cup diced red onion
1 cup pineapple chunks, drained. Reserve juice.
1 (8 ounce) can sliced water chestnuts, drained
½ cup reserved pineapple juice
2 tablespoons hoisin sauce
1 teaspoon soy sauce
1 (16 ounce) can of sweet and sour sauce

DIRECTIONS

1. In a bowl, combine the sweet & sour sauce, soy sauce, hoisin sauce, and pineapple juice.
2. Place the chicken and remaining ingredients in the cooker and pour the sauce over.
3. Close the lid and set the valve to the STEAM position.
4. Slow Cook on LOW 6 hours.
5. Serve over hot rice.

Slow Cooked Pulled-Pork Wraps

INGREDIENTS

For pulled pork:

2 ½ pound boneless pork butt or shoulder, trimmed of excess fat
1 (14½ ounce) can petite diced tomatoes
1 large onion, chopped
1 teaspoon garlic powder
1 teaspoon salt
2 teaspoons cumin powder
1 tablespoon jalapeño rings
2 tablespoons dried oregano, rubbed between the palms
2 tablespoons unsweetened cocoa powder
1 lime, juiced

For tacos:

20 corn tortillas
1 bunch fresh cilantro, finely chopped
1 cup sour cream (or plain yogurt)

SLOW COOK

DIRECTIONS

1. Add the tomatoes, onion, salt, cumin, jalapeños, oregano, and cocoa powder into the cooker and mix well to combine.
2. Lower the roast in the cooker and coat the tomato mixture on all sides of the roast.
3. Close the lid and set the valve to the STEAM position.
4. Slow Cook on HIGH 4-5 hours.
5. When time is up, shred the meat with two forks – mixing it back into the sauce - and squirt with lime juice.
6. Serve on warmed corn tortillas with a sprinkle of cilantro and a dollop of sour cream.

Recipe Tip:
If you're not a fan of spicy foods, you can omit the jalapeños.

Slow Cooker Zucchini & Tomato Lasagna

A healthy take on a classic dish, get all the flavor of lasagna with less guilt.

Slow Cooking Time
3 hours HIGH or 5-6 hours LOW

Serves
4 - 6

INGREDIENTS

1 tablespoon olive oil
24 ounces prepared tomato sauce
2 cups Mozzarella or Provolone cheese, grated
16 ounces ricotta cheese
3 pinches salt
16 ounces zucchini (about three medium zucchini), grated
For garnish: grated Parmigiano Reggiano cheese and torn basil leaves

DIRECTIONS

1. Pour a tablespoon of olive oil into the cooker, and using a paper towel spread the oil all over the base and up the sides of the cooker.
2. Pour in ½ cup of the sauce and pull out and shake the insert to even it out into an even layer. Make the first layer of lasagna strips, overlapping and breaking them as needed to fill in the holes on the edges as needed, and press into the tomato sauce.
3. Make the first layer by sprinkling half a handful of mozzarella strips, dotting the ricotta, sprinkling the salt, distributing the zucchini, dotting the tomato sauce, and sprinkling another half handful of mozzarella on top.
4. Press another layer of lasagna strips, changing the orientation, and make two more layers as stated in the previous step (mozzarella, ricotta, salt, zucchini, tomato sauce, mozzarella) – reserve a handful of mozzarella to use at the end.
5. Finish the layering by covering with lasagna strips and pouring the remaining tomato sauce on top. Close the lid and set the valve to the STEAM position.
6. Slow Cook on HIGH for 3 hours or on LOW for 5-6 hours. When time is up remove the lid and sprinkle with the remaining mozzarella – let stand uncovered for 30 minutes before serving.
7. Slice with a spatula and pull out the slices using a spoon. Optionally garnish with Parmesan cheese and basil leaves before serving.

Recipe Tip:
If you prefer pasta, you can use any kind of Lasagna strips for this recipe – gluten-free, whole wheat, pre-cooked, or those that need pre-cooking.

Super Easy Short Ribs – Barbecue Style

INGREDIENTS

3 pounds boneless beef short ribs
1 large onion, thinly sliced
1 cup prepared barbecue sauce
1 cup water
1 teaspoon garlic powder
Salt and black pepper, to taste

DIRECTIONS

1. Season the meat with salt and pepper and brown in the cooker. It may be necessary to do this in 2 batches.
2. Return all of the meat to the cooker and stir in onion and garlic powder.
3. Combine the barbecue sauce and water and add to the cooker.
4. Close the lid and set the valve to the STEAM position.
5. Slow Cook on LOW for 8 hours.

Recipe Tip:
Try this recipe with any flavor BBQ sauce for added variety.

Beef Fajitas

Slow Cooking Time
5.5 hours LOW

Serves
6

SLOW COOK

INGREDIENTS

¾ cup salsa
2 tablespoons tomato paste
1 tablespoon olive oil
1 clove garlic, minced
3 tablespoons lime juice
1 teaspoon black pepper
½ teaspoon salt
1½ pounds flank steak, trimmed
1 large onion, cut in half and thinly sliced into half-moons
2 red bell peppers cut into strips
1 package flour tortillas
Guacamole (optional)
Tomatoes, chopped (optional)

DIRECTIONS

1. In a small bowl, combine salsa, tomato paste, olive oil, garlic, lime juice, pepper, and salt.
2. Lay the flank steak in the cooker and pour the mixture over it, making sure to coat all exposed surfaces thoroughly.
3. Lay the onion and bell peppers on top.
4. Close the lid and set the valve to the STEAM position.
5. Slow Cook on LOW for 5½ hours.
6. Remove the steak and vegetables from the juice and transfer to a serving platter.
7. Cover with aluminum foil and let stand 10 minutes.
8. Cut the meat across the grain into ½-inch thick slices. Serve it with warm tortillas, the peppers, and onions. Garnish with guacamole and chopped tomatoes.

Hands-free French Toast

This recipe also works well with gluten-free and whole wheat breads – you can also mix the bread types if you like.

Slow Cooking Time
2 hours HIGH or 4-5 hours LOW

Serves
6 - 8

INGREDIENTS

1 teaspoon olive oil
6 medium eggs
2 cups milk (your favorite kind)
2 teaspoons vanilla extract
1 teaspoon cinnamon powder
1½ pounds French bread, sliced into half-rounds.
4 tablespoons butter, chopped
2-4 tablespoons brown sugar

DIRECTIONS

1. Pour the olive oil in the cooker base, and using a paper towel spread the oil all over the bottom and up half-way of the sides.
2. In a large bowl add the eggs, milk, vanilla, and cinnamon and mix well. Drop in the bread cubes in the mixture and gently mix well. Let stand for 15 minutes, lightly mixing every five minutes.
3. Pour the bread and egg mixture into the cooker, encouraging it to go in an even layer. Pour any remaining batter from the bowl on top. Dot the top with butter and sprinkle on the brown sugar.
4. Close the lid and set the valve to the STEAM position.
5. Slow Cook on HIGH for 2 hours or LOW 4-5 hours.
6. Once done, let stand, uncovered, for 10 minutes before serving along with a bottle of your favorite maple syrup.

Recipe Tip:
If your multi-cooker has multiple inserts, use the ceramic-coated or non-stick one. This recipe will still work in a stainless steel insert, but unfortunately, the eggs will most likely stick to the base.

Crust-less Apple Pie a la mode

Slow Cooking Time
2 hours HIGH or 6 hours LOW

Serves
4 - 6

INGREDIENTS

2 – 2½ pounds apples (any kind), cored, and cut into ¼-inch-thick slices
⅓ cup brown sugar or muscovado sugar
1 tablespoon cornstarch
1 teaspoon ground cinnamon
¼ teaspoon ground nutmeg
1 pound vanilla ice cream

DIRECTIONS

1. Put the apples in the cooker as you slice them.
2. Then add the, brown sugar, cornstarch, cinnamon, and nutmeg in a slow cooker and mix well.
3. Close the lid and set the valve to the STEAM position.
4. Slow Cook on HIGH for 2 hours or on LOW for 6 hours.
5. Serve warm in small dessert bowls and top with a scoop of vanilla ice cream.

Easy Mocha Fudge Brownie Cake

INGREDIENTS

4 large eggs
1 cup white sugar
½ cup olive oil
1 tablespoon vanilla extract
1 cup all-purpose flour
½ cup un-sweetened cocoa powder
1 tablespoon instant coffee granules
¼ teaspoon salt
¼ cup toasted walnuts

DIRECTIONS

1. Add a large square of parchment paper into the cooker and press well into the shape of the base (with the sides sticking up).
2. In a large bowl, mix the eggs, sugar, oil, and vanilla until blended. Sprinkle in the flour, cocoa, coffee granules, and salt and mix well.
3. Close the lid and set the valve to the STEAM position.
4. Slow Cook on LOW for 3 hours or until a toothpick comes out with moist crumbs.
5. Lift the cake out of the cooker, slice into squares, and sprinkle with walnuts before serving.

INDEX